PRIMARY MATHEMATICS 6B
TEXTBOOK

Marshall Cavendish
Education

US Distributor

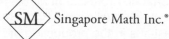
SM Singapore Math Inc.®

Original edition published under the title Primary Mathematics Textbook 6B

© 1985 Curriculum Planning & Development Division
Ministry of Education, Singapore
Published by Times Media Private Limited
This American Edition
© 2003 Marshall Cavendish International (Singapore) Private Limited
© 2014 Marshall Cavendish Education Pte Ltd

Published by Marshall Cavendish Education
Times Centre, 1 New Industrial Road, Singapore 536196
Customer Service Hotline: (65) 6213 9444
US Office Tel: (1-914) 332 8888 | Fax: (1-914) 332 8882
E-mail: tmesales@mceducation.com
Website: www.mceducation.com

First published 2003
Second impression 2003
Third impression 2005
Reprinted 2006 (twice), 2008, 2009 (twice), 2010, 2012, 2014, 2015, 2017

Singapore Math Inc.®
Distributed by
Singapore Math Inc.®
19535 SW 129th Avenue
Tualatin, OR 97062
U.S.A.
Website: www.singaporemath.com

ISBN 978-981-01-8515-2

Printed in Singapore

ACKNOWLEDGEMENTS

Our special thanks to Richard Askey, Professor of Mathematics (University of Wisconsin,
Madison), Yoram Sagher, Professor of Mathematics (University of Illinois, Chicago), and Madge
Goldman, President (Gabriella and Paul Rosenbaum Foundation), for their indispensable
advice and suggestions in the production of Primary Mathematics (U.S. Edition).

PREFACE

Primary Mathematics (U.S. Edition) comprises textbooks and workbooks. The main feature of this package is the use of the **Concrete ➡ Pictorial ➡ Abstract** approach. The students are provided with the necessary learning experiences beginning with the concrete and pictorial stages, followed by the abstract stage to enable them to learn mathematics meaningfully. This package encourages active thinking processes, communication of mathematical ideas and problem solving.

This textbook comprises 6 units. Each unit is divided into parts: ❶, ❷, . . . Each part starts with a meaningful situation for communication and is followed by specific learning tasks numbered 1, 2, . . . The textbook is accompanied by a workbook. The sign ⌐Workbook Exercise⌐> is used to link the textbook to the workbook exercises.

Practice exercises are designed to provide the students with further practice after they have done the relevant workbook exercises. Review exercises are provided for cumulative reviews of concepts and skills. All the practice exercises and review exercises are optional exercises.

The color patch ■ is used to invite active participation from the students and to facilitate oral discussion. The students are advised not to write on the color patches.

Challenging word problems are marked with *. Teachers may encourage the abler students to attempt them.

CONTENTS

1 Fractions

① Division

Azizah bought 3 oranges. She cut each orange into halves. How many pieces of orange did she have?

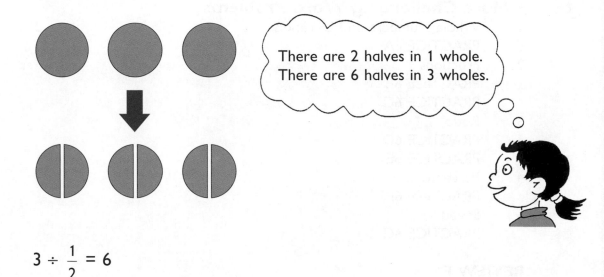

There are 2 halves in 1 whole.
There are 6 halves in 3 wholes.

$$3 \div \frac{1}{2} = 6$$

She had 6 pieces of orange.

$$3 \div \frac{1}{2} = 3 \times 2$$
$$= 6$$

Dividing by $\frac{1}{2}$ is the same as multiplying by 2.

1. Divide 2 by $\frac{1}{3}$.

$2 \div \frac{1}{3} = 2 \times 3$

$\qquad = \blacksquare$

How many thirds are there in 2 wholes?

2. Divide.

(a) $1 \div \frac{1}{4} = 1 \times \blacksquare$

$\qquad = \blacksquare$

(b) $2 \div \frac{1}{5} = 2 \times \blacksquare$

$\qquad = \blacksquare$

3. Divide.

(a) $4 \div \frac{1}{2}$

(b) $6 \div \frac{1}{6}$

(c) $3 \div \frac{1}{7}$

(d) $8 \div \frac{1}{4}$

(e) $5 \div \frac{1}{3}$

(f) $9 \div \frac{1}{9}$

Workbook Exercise 1

4. Divide $\frac{1}{2}$ by 4.

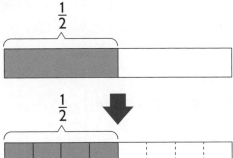

Divide $\frac{1}{2}$ into 4 equal parts.

Each part is $\frac{1}{8}$.

$\frac{1}{2} \div 4 = \frac{1}{2} \times \frac{1}{4}$

$\qquad = \blacksquare$

Dividing by 4 is the same as multiplying by $\frac{1}{4}$.

5. Divide.

(a) $\dfrac{1}{3} \div 2 = \dfrac{1}{3} \times \blacksquare$

$= \blacksquare$

(b) $\dfrac{4}{5} \div 8 = \dfrac{4}{5} \times \blacksquare$

$= \blacksquare$

6. Divide.

(a) $\dfrac{1}{2} \div 3$

(b) $\dfrac{1}{4} \div 6$

(c) $\dfrac{1}{6} \div 5$

(d) $\dfrac{2}{3} \div 3$

(e) $\dfrac{2}{7} \div 2$

(f) $\dfrac{4}{9} \div 8$

Workbook Exercise 2

7. Divide $\dfrac{1}{2}$ by $\dfrac{1}{4}$.

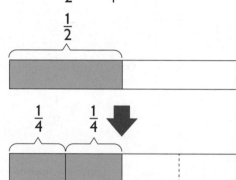

Divide $\dfrac{1}{2}$ into quarters.

There are 2 quarters.

$\dfrac{1}{2} \div \dfrac{1}{4} = \dfrac{1}{2} \times 4$

$= \blacksquare$

Dividing by $\dfrac{1}{4}$ is the same as multiplying by 4.

8. Divide.

(a) $\dfrac{2}{3} \div \dfrac{1}{3} = \dfrac{2}{3} \times \blacksquare$

$= \blacksquare$

(b) $\dfrac{2}{3} \div \dfrac{1}{6} = \dfrac{2}{3} \times \blacksquare$

$= \blacksquare$

9. Divide.

(a) $\dfrac{1}{4} \div \dfrac{1}{2}$

(b) $\dfrac{2}{5} \div \dfrac{1}{10}$

(c) $\dfrac{3}{4} \div \dfrac{1}{8}$

(d) $\dfrac{5}{6} \div \dfrac{1}{6}$

(e) $\dfrac{2}{9} \div \dfrac{1}{3}$

(f) $\dfrac{3}{8} \div \dfrac{1}{4}$

10. Divide 3 by $\frac{3}{4}$.

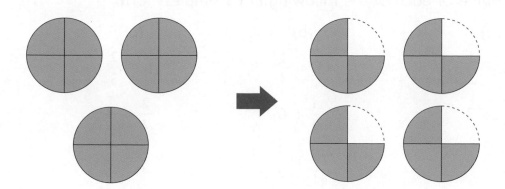

$3 \div \frac{3}{4} = 3 \times \frac{4}{3}$

$\qquad = \blacksquare$

How many $\frac{3}{4}$'s can be made from 3 wholes?

Dividing by $\frac{3}{4}$ is the same as multiplying by $\frac{4}{3}$.

11. Divide.

(a) $1 \div \frac{3}{8} = 1 \times \blacksquare$

$\qquad = \blacksquare$

(b) $2 \div \frac{4}{5} = 2 \times \blacksquare$

$\qquad = \blacksquare$

(c) $\frac{1}{3} \div \frac{2}{9} = \frac{1}{3} \times \blacksquare$

$\qquad = \blacksquare$

(d) $\frac{5}{6} \div \frac{2}{3} = \frac{5}{6} \times \blacksquare$

$\qquad = \blacksquare$

12. Divide.

(a) $3 \div \frac{2}{3}$

(b) $6 \div \frac{3}{5}$

(c) $4 \div \frac{6}{7}$

(d) $\frac{2}{3} \div \frac{3}{5}$

(e) $\frac{3}{5} \div \frac{9}{10}$

(f) $\frac{5}{8} \div \frac{2}{5}$

Workbook Exercise 3

PRACTICE 1A

Find the value of each of the following in its simplest form.

	(a)	(b)	(c)
1.	$3 \div \dfrac{1}{2}$	$5 \div \dfrac{1}{4}$	$6 \div \dfrac{2}{3}$
2.	$\dfrac{1}{5} \div 2$	$\dfrac{1}{2} \div 6$	$\dfrac{2}{7} \div 4$
3.	$\dfrac{1}{4} \div \dfrac{1}{2}$	$\dfrac{8}{9} \div \dfrac{1}{3}$	$\dfrac{3}{4} \div \dfrac{1}{6}$
4.	$\dfrac{1}{6} \div \dfrac{2}{3}$	$\dfrac{3}{4} \div \dfrac{9}{10}$	$\dfrac{4}{5} \div \dfrac{5}{8}$

5. (a) How many $\dfrac{1}{6}$'s are there in 3?

   (b) How many $\dfrac{1}{6}$'s are there in $\dfrac{2}{3}$?

6. How many $\dfrac{1}{2}$-hour periods will make up 4 hours?

7. How many bricks weighing $\dfrac{1}{4}$ lb each will have a total weight of 3 lb?

8. How many pieces of string, each $\dfrac{1}{5}$ m long, can be cut from a string 3 m long?

9. Nicole used 6 m of string to tie some packages. She used $\dfrac{2}{3}$ m of string for each package. How many packages did she tie?

10. Holly had 2 kg of beef. She used $\dfrac{4}{5}$ of it to make stew. How many kilograms of beef did she have left?

11. Kimberly cuts 6 pieces of tape, each $\dfrac{4}{5}$ m long, from a roll of tape 5 m long. How many meters of tape are left in the roll?

② Order of Operations

Find the value of $\frac{1}{4} + \frac{3}{4} \times 4$.

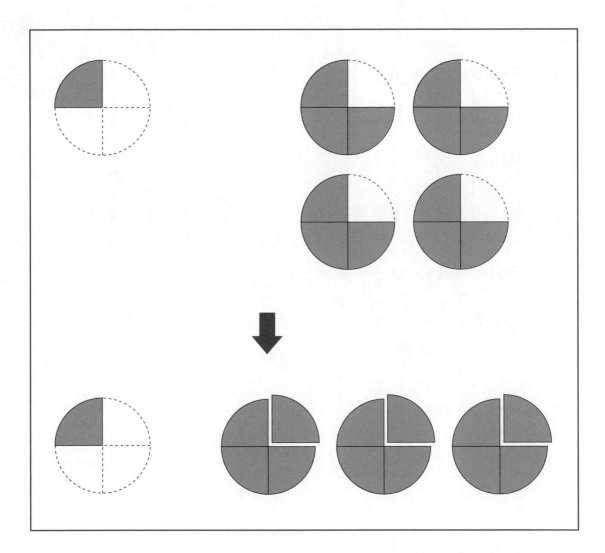

$\frac{1}{4} + \frac{3}{4} \times 4$

$= \frac{1}{4} + \blacksquare$

$= \blacksquare$

Do multiplication first.

1. Find the value of $\dfrac{3}{4} - \dfrac{1}{2} + \dfrac{1}{3}$.

$$\dfrac{3}{4} - \dfrac{1}{2} + \dfrac{1}{3} = \dfrac{9}{12} - \dfrac{6}{12} + \dfrac{4}{12}$$

$$= \dfrac{\blacksquare}{12}$$

12 is a common multiple of 4, 2 and 3.

2. Find the value of

   (a) $\dfrac{1}{3} + \dfrac{3}{4} + \dfrac{1}{2}$

   (b) $\dfrac{1}{3} + \dfrac{5}{6} - \dfrac{3}{4}$

   (c) $\dfrac{1}{5} + \dfrac{7}{10} - \dfrac{3}{4}$

   (d) $\dfrac{8}{9} - \dfrac{1}{6} - \dfrac{1}{2}$

   (e) $\dfrac{1}{2} - \dfrac{2}{5} + \dfrac{3}{10}$

   (f) $\dfrac{5}{8} - \dfrac{1}{2} + \dfrac{3}{4}$

3. Find the value of $\dfrac{7}{9} \times 5 \times \dfrac{3}{8}$.

$$\dfrac{7}{\cancel{9}_3} \times 5 \times \dfrac{\cancel{3}^1}{8} = \dfrac{7 \times 5}{3 \times 8}$$

$$= \blacksquare$$

4. Find the value of $\dfrac{2}{5} \times \dfrac{3}{4} \div \dfrac{1}{2}$.

$$\dfrac{2}{5} \times \dfrac{3}{4} \div \dfrac{1}{2} = \dfrac{2}{5} \times \dfrac{3}{4} \times 2$$

$$= \blacksquare$$

5. Find the value of $\dfrac{9}{10} \div \dfrac{3}{5} \times \dfrac{2}{3}$.

$$\dfrac{9}{10} \div \dfrac{3}{5} \times \dfrac{2}{3} = \dfrac{9}{10} \times \dfrac{5}{3} \times \dfrac{2}{3}$$

$$= \blacksquare$$

6. Find the value of $\dfrac{5}{6} \div \dfrac{1}{2} \div 4$.

$$\dfrac{5}{6} \div \dfrac{1}{2} \div 4 = \dfrac{5}{6} \times 2 \times \dfrac{1}{4}$$

$$= \blacksquare$$

7. Find the value of

(a) $3 \times \dfrac{1}{2} \times \dfrac{5}{6}$

(b) $\dfrac{1}{3} \times \dfrac{3}{4} \times 8$

(c) $\dfrac{4}{9} \div 4 \div \dfrac{3}{5}$

(d) $\dfrac{3}{8} \div \dfrac{1}{2} \div 3$

(e) $14 \div 2 \times \dfrac{2}{7}$

(f) $\dfrac{3}{5} \times \dfrac{4}{9} \div \dfrac{3}{10}$

Workbook Exercise 4

8. Find the value of $4 + 6 \times \dfrac{5}{8}$.

$$4 + 6 \times \dfrac{5}{8} = 4 + \blacksquare$$

$$= \blacksquare$$

Do multiplication or division from left to right, then addition or subtraction from left to right.

9. Find the value of $1 - \dfrac{4}{5} \div 6$.

$$1 - \dfrac{4}{5} \div 6 = 1 - \blacksquare$$

$$= \blacksquare$$

10. Find the value of

(a) $3 - \dfrac{1}{3} \div 4$

(b) $7 + 5 \times \dfrac{9}{10}$

(c) $4 \div \dfrac{2}{5} + 5 \div \dfrac{5}{8}$

(d) $8 \times 4 - 6 \div \dfrac{2}{3}$

(e) $2 \times 3 \div 9 + \dfrac{1}{2}$

(f) $4 \div 6 \times 6 + \dfrac{2}{5}$

11. Find the value of $\frac{3}{8} - \frac{3}{4} \times \frac{1}{3}$.

$$\frac{3}{8} - \frac{3}{4} \times \frac{1}{3} = \frac{3}{8} - \blacksquare$$

$$= \blacksquare$$

12. Find the value of $\frac{5}{6} + \frac{2}{3} \div 4 \times \frac{1}{2}$.

$$\frac{5}{6} + \frac{2}{3} \div 4 \times \frac{1}{2} = \frac{5}{6} + \blacksquare$$

$$= \blacksquare$$

13. Find the value of

(a) $\frac{3}{4} + \frac{2}{5} \times \frac{1}{4}$

(b) $\frac{3}{5} - \frac{3}{4} \times \frac{2}{9}$

(c) $\frac{1}{8} + \frac{1}{2} \div \frac{1}{4}$

(d) $\frac{7}{9} - \frac{1}{5} \div \frac{3}{10}$

(e) $\frac{2}{3} + \frac{5}{6} \div 10 \times \frac{2}{3}$

(f) $\frac{5}{8} - \frac{5}{8} \times \frac{4}{5} \div 2$

Workbook Exercise 5

14. Find the value of $(\frac{4}{5} - \frac{1}{2}) \div 4$.

$$(\frac{4}{5} - \frac{1}{2}) \div 4 = \blacksquare \div 4$$

$$= \blacksquare$$

Do what is in the parenthesis first.

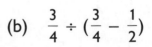

15. Find the value of

(a) $(\frac{3}{5} + \frac{1}{3}) \div \frac{2}{5}$

(b) $\frac{3}{4} \div (\frac{3}{4} - \frac{1}{2})$

(c) $\frac{4}{7} \times (\frac{3}{4} + \frac{1}{8})$

(d) $(\frac{1}{3} + \frac{5}{12}) \times \frac{4}{9}$

(e) $\frac{2}{3} \times (\frac{1}{2} + \frac{1}{4}) - \frac{3}{8}$

(f) $\frac{2}{5} + (\frac{1}{3} + \frac{1}{2}) \div \frac{3}{4}$

Workbook Exercise 6

PRACTICE 1B

Find the value of each of the following in its simplest form.

1.   (a) $\dfrac{2}{3} + \dfrac{1}{4} - \dfrac{1}{2}$ (b) $\dfrac{7}{8} - \dfrac{1}{4} + \dfrac{1}{2}$

    (c) $2 \times \dfrac{4}{9} \div \dfrac{2}{3}$ (d) $\dfrac{3}{5} \div 6 \times \dfrac{5}{6}$

    (e) $\dfrac{3}{4} \times \dfrac{2}{3} \div \dfrac{1}{2}$ (f) $\dfrac{5}{6} \div \dfrac{3}{4} \div \dfrac{5}{9}$

2.   (a) $6 + 4 \times \dfrac{3}{4}$ (b) $\dfrac{3}{4} \times 8 - 6 \times \dfrac{2}{3}$

    (c) $3 + 6 \div \dfrac{2}{7}$ (d) $\dfrac{5}{6} \div 10 + 2$

    (e) $2 + \dfrac{8}{9} \div \dfrac{2}{3}$ (f) $7 - \dfrac{9}{10} \div \dfrac{3}{5}$

3.   (a) $6 \times (1 - \dfrac{3}{4})$ (b) $(\dfrac{3}{4} - \dfrac{1}{2}) \div 3$

    (c) $\dfrac{2}{5} \times (\dfrac{3}{4} - \dfrac{3}{8})$ (d) $(\dfrac{1}{4} + \dfrac{3}{8}) \div \dfrac{5}{6}$

    (e) $\dfrac{4}{9} \div (2 \div \dfrac{3}{4})$ (f) $\dfrac{1}{7} \div (\dfrac{1}{3} \times \dfrac{6}{7})$

4.   (a) $(20 - 8) \times \dfrac{3}{4} \div 3$ (b) $(8 + 4) \div \dfrac{1}{2} \times \dfrac{5}{6}$

    (c) $(20 + 12) \div 12 \times \dfrac{3}{8}$ (d) $(12 + 4) \div \dfrac{4}{5} \div 8$

    (e) $\dfrac{3}{8} \times (\dfrac{5}{6} - \dfrac{1}{2}) \times \dfrac{2}{5}$ (f) $\dfrac{2}{3} \div \dfrac{4}{9} \div (\dfrac{1}{2} - \dfrac{3}{8})$

5.   (a) $8 - 6 \times \dfrac{2}{3} \div 2$ (b) $16 - 4 \times 2 + 4 \div \dfrac{1}{2}$

    (c) $\dfrac{2}{5} \times (18 - 3) + \dfrac{3}{10}$ (d) $\dfrac{4}{5} - (\dfrac{3}{4} - \dfrac{2}{3}) \times 2$

    (e) $(\dfrac{5}{6} - \dfrac{3}{4}) \div \dfrac{2}{3} + \dfrac{3}{4}$ (f) $\dfrac{5}{9} \div \dfrac{5}{6} - \dfrac{4}{5} \times \dfrac{3}{4}$

15

③ Word Problems

A tank is $\frac{1}{5}$ full. When another 700 ml of water is poured into the tank, it becomes $\frac{2}{3}$ full.

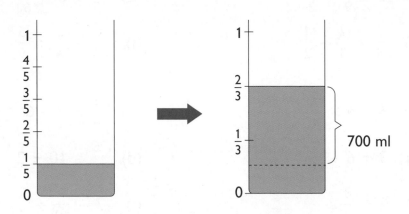

$$\frac{2}{3} - \frac{1}{5} = \frac{10}{15} - \frac{3}{15}$$
$$= \frac{7}{15}$$

700 ml fills $\frac{7}{15}$ of the tank.

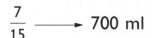 700 ml

How much water is in the tank when it is $\frac{1}{5}$ full?

$\frac{1}{5}$ ⟶ ■ ml

How much water is in the tank when it is $\frac{2}{3}$ full?

$\frac{2}{3}$ ⟶ ■ ml

16

1. Alex bought some chairs. $\frac{1}{3}$ of them were red and $\frac{1}{4}$ were blue.
   The remaining 35 chairs were yellow.
   (a) What fraction of the chairs were yellow?

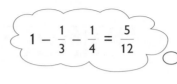

$$1 - \frac{1}{3} - \frac{1}{4} = \frac{5}{12}$$

   (b) How many chairs did Alex buy?

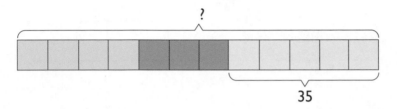

?

35

2. Max spent $\frac{3}{5}$ of his money in a shop and $\frac{1}{4}$ of the remainder in another shop.

   (a) What fraction of his money was left?

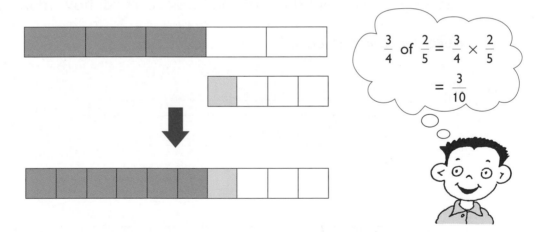

$$\frac{3}{4} \text{ of } \frac{2}{5} = \frac{3}{4} \times \frac{2}{5}$$
$$= \frac{3}{10}$$

   (b) If he had $90 left, how much money did he have at first?

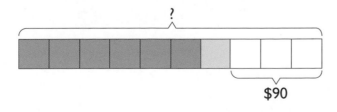

?

$90

Workbook Exercise 7

3. Megan spent $\frac{2}{5}$ of her money on a doll and $\frac{1}{2}$ of the remainder on a musical box. She spent $8 more on the doll than on the musical box. How much money did she have left?

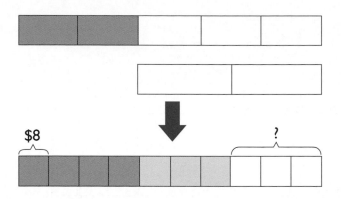

4. Lindsey read $\frac{2}{5}$ of a book on Monday. She read 12 pages on Tuesday. If she still had $\frac{1}{2}$ of the book to read, how many pages were there in the book?

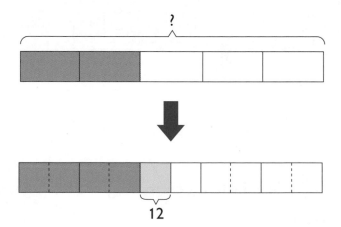

1 unit = 12

10 units = ■

5. $\frac{1}{4}$ of the beads in a box are red. There are 24 more yellow beads than red beads. The remaining 76 beads are blue. How many beads are there altogether?

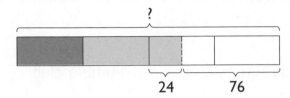

$\frac{1}{2}$ ⟶ 24 + 76 = 100 beads

1 ⟶ 200 beads

There are 200 beads altogether.

6. 10 jugs of water can fill $\frac{5}{8}$ of a bucket. Another 4 jugs and 5 cups of water are needed to fill the remaining part of the bucket. How many cups of water can the bucket hold?

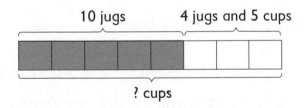

$\frac{5}{8}$ ⟶ 10 jugs

$\frac{1}{8}$ ⟶ 2 jugs

$\frac{2}{8}$ ⟶ 4 jugs

$\frac{1}{8}$ ⟶ 5 cups

1 ⟶ 40 cups

The bucket can hold 40 cups of water.

Workbook Exercise 8

PRACTICE 1C

1. There are 300 passengers on board an airplane. $\frac{2}{3}$ of them are men, $\frac{1}{4}$ are women and the rest are children. How many children are there?

2. There are 350 members in a swimming club. $\frac{2}{7}$ of them are new members. $\frac{3}{10}$ of the new members are females. How many new female members are there?

3. Sally made 500 cookies. She sold $\frac{3}{4}$ of them and gave away $\frac{2}{5}$ of the remainder. How many cookies did she give away?

4. Dani made some sticks of satay for a party. $\frac{3}{5}$ of them were chicken satay and the rest were beef satay. There were 240 sticks of beef satay. How many sticks of chicken satay were there?

5. After paying $30 for a shirt, David had $\frac{3}{5}$ of his money left. How much money did he have at first?

6. After spending $\frac{2}{5}$ of his money on a storybook, Mathew had $12 left. How much did he spend on the storybook?

7. Greg spent $\frac{1}{4}$ of his money on a typewriter. If the typewriter cost $120, how much money did he have at first?

8. Cameron has 480 stamps. $\frac{5}{8}$ of them are U.S. stamps and the rest are foreign stamps. How many more U.S. stamps than foreign stamps does he have?

9. Taylor bought 24 lb of flour. She used $\frac{1}{3}$ of it to bake cookies and $\frac{1}{4}$ of the remainder to bake a cake. How many pounds of flour were left?

PRACTICE 1D

1. Ryan withdrew $\frac{1}{4}$ of his savings from the bank. He spent $450 of it and had $150 left. How much was his total savings in the bank at first?

2. After giving $\frac{1}{3}$ of his money to his wife and $\frac{1}{4}$ of it to his mother, Jake still had $600 left. How much money did he give to his mother?

3. Lucy spent $\frac{3}{5}$ of her money on a handbag. She spent the remainder on 3 T-shirts which cost $4 each. How much did the handbag cost?

4. Merisa spent $\frac{3}{4}$ of her money on a dictionary. She spent $\frac{1}{2}$ of the remainder on a calculator. The dictionary cost $30 more than the calculator. How much did the dictionary cost?

5. Jake made some tarts. He sold $\frac{3}{5}$ of them and gave $\frac{1}{4}$ of the remainder to his friends. If he had 150 tarts left, how many tarts did he sell?

6. Susan spent $\frac{1}{4}$ of her money on a storybook and $\frac{1}{2}$ of the remainder on a box of crayons. She spent $10 altogether. How much money did she have left?

7. Michael bought a shirt with $\frac{2}{5}$ of his money. Then he bought a jacket which cost $5 more than the shirt. He spent $105 altogether. How much money did he have left?

8. Wendy spends $\frac{3}{5}$ of her money on 3 bowls and 8 plates. With the rest of her money, she can buy another 6 bowls. If she spends all her money on plates only, how many plates can she buy?

2 Circles

① Radius and Diameter

Draw a circle using a pair of compasses.

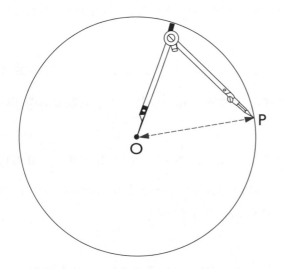

O is the **center** of the circle.
OP is a **radius** of the circle.

Then draw a straight line MP which passes through the center of the circle.

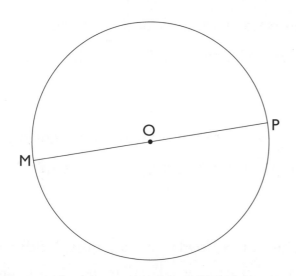

MP is a **diameter** of the circle.

Is MP twice as long as OP?

1. Measure the radius of each circle.

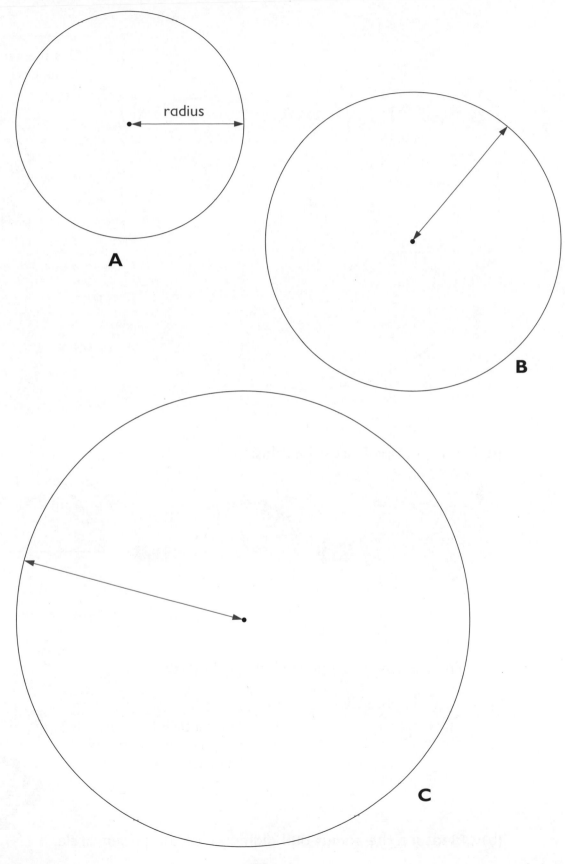

radius

A

B

C

2. Measure the radius and diameter of the circle.

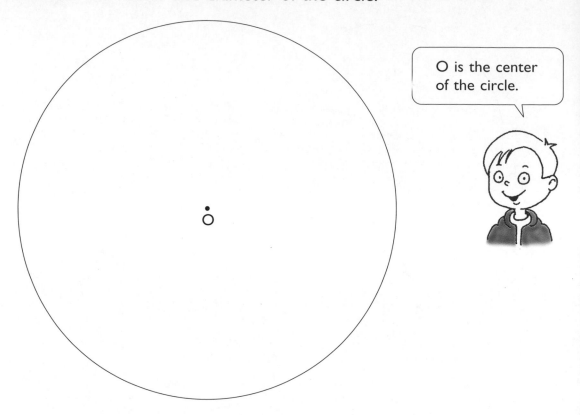

O is the center of the circle.

3. (a) Fold a paper circle like this:

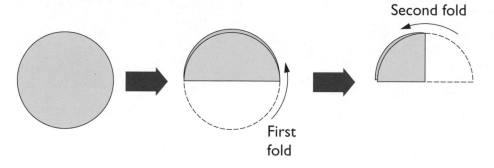

Second fold

First fold

Then unfold the paper circle to find its center.

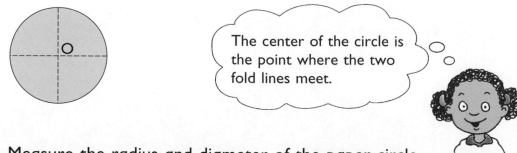

The center of the circle is the point where the two fold lines meet.

(b) Measure the radius and diameter of the paper circle.

$$\boxed{\text{Diameter} = 2 \times \text{Radius}}$$
$$\text{Radius} = \text{Diameter} \div 2$$

4. Draw a circle of radius 5 cm.

5. Draw a circle of diameter 8 cm.

6. (a) The radius of the circle is 4 cm.
        Find its diameter.

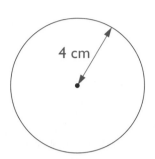

(b) The diameter of the circle is 18 cm.
        Find its radius.

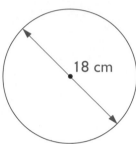

7. The following circles are not drawn to scale.

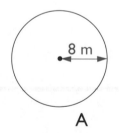 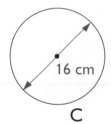 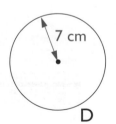

| A | B | C | D |

(a) Which circle is the biggest?
(b) Which circle is the smallest?
(c) Copy and complete the table:

Circle	Radius	Diameter
A	8 m	
B		20 m
C		16 cm
D	7 cm	

Workbook Exercise 9

② Circumference

Use a string to measure the **circumference** of a circle like this:

> The **circumference** of a circle is its perimeter.

> The circumference of a circle is slightly more than 3 times its diameter.

1. Aziz measured the diameter and the circumference of three circles. He recorded the results as follows:

Circle	Diameter	Circumference
A	5 cm	15.7 cm
B	7 cm	22 cm
C	10 cm	31.4 cm

Find the value of **circumference ÷ diameter** for each circle. What do you notice?

> The circumference of each circle is about 3.14 times the diameter.

The value of **circumference ÷ diameter** is the same for any circle. This value is represented by π.

$\pi \approx 3.14$ or $\dfrac{22}{7}$

Circumference of circle $= \pi \times$ Diameter

2. The diameter of a hoop is 60 cm. Find its circumference.
(Take $\pi = 3.14$)

Circumference $= \pi \times 60$

$= 3.14 \times 60$

$= \blacksquare$ cm

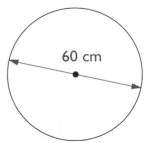

60 cm

3. The radius of a disc is 25 cm. Find its circumference. (Take π = 3.14)

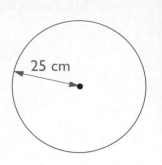

Diameter = 2 × 25

    = 50 cm

Circumference = π × 50

    = 3.14 × 50

    = ■ cm

4. The radius of a wheel is 14 cm. Find its circumference.

$\left(\text{Take } \pi = \dfrac{22}{7}\right)$

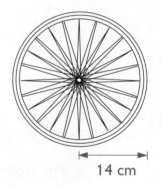

Diameter = 28 cm

Circumference = π × 28

    = $\dfrac{22}{7}$ × 28

    = ■ cm

5. Find the circumference of a circle of diameter 70 cm. $\left(\text{Take } \pi = \dfrac{22}{7}\right)$

6. Find the circumference of a circle of radius 4 m. (Take π = 3.14)

7. Find the circumference of each circle. $\left(\text{Take } \pi = \dfrac{22}{7}\right)$

(a)

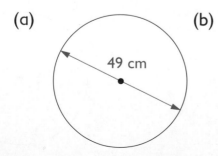

49 cm

(b)

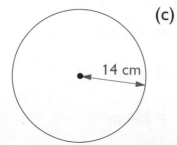

14 cm

(c)

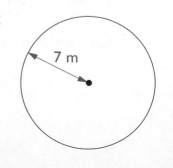

7 m

8. Find the circumference of each circle. (Take $\pi = 3.14$)

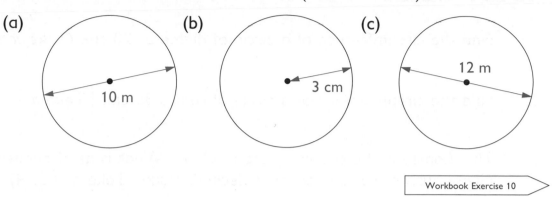

(a) 10 m

(b) 3 cm

(c) 12 m

Workbook Exercise 10

9. The figure shows a flowerbed which has the shape of a **semicircle**. Find its perimeter. (Take $\pi = 3.14$)

A **semicircle** is a half circle.

4 m

10. A wire is bent to form three semicircles as shown. Find the length of the wire in terms of π.

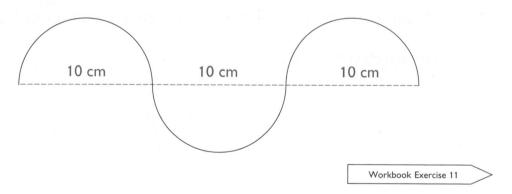

10 cm   10 cm   10 cm

Workbook Exercise 11

11. The figure is made up of a rectangle and two semicircles. Find its perimeter. $\left(\text{Take } \pi = \dfrac{22}{7}\right)$

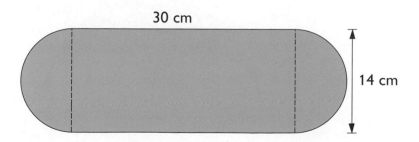

30 cm

14 cm

PRACTICE 2A

1. Find the circumference of a circle of diameter 20 cm. (Take π = 3.14)

2. Find the circumference of a circle of radius 35 cm. $\left(\text{Take } \pi = \dfrac{22}{7}\right)$

3. The diameter of a circular plate is 23 cm. What is its circumference? Give your answer correct to 1 decimal place. (Take π = 3.14)

4. The figure shows a circle within a square. Find the circumference of the circle. (Take π = 3.14)

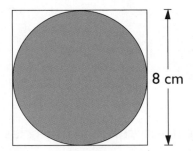

8 cm

5. What is the length of this curve which is made up of four equal semicircles? $\left(\text{Take } \pi = \dfrac{22}{7}\right)$

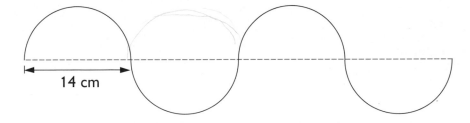

14 cm

6. The figure is made up of 3 semicircles. Find its perimeter in terms of π.

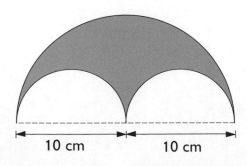

10 cm   10 cm

③ Area

The radius of the circle is 10 cm. Estimate its area.

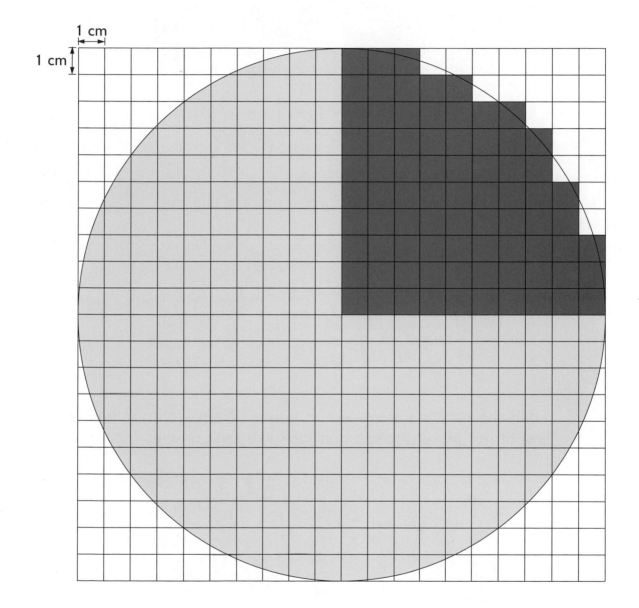

Area of $\frac{1}{4}$ of the circle $\approx$ 79 cm²

Area of the circle $\approx$ 4 × 79

$= 316$ cm²

1. Eva cut a circle into 24 equal pieces.

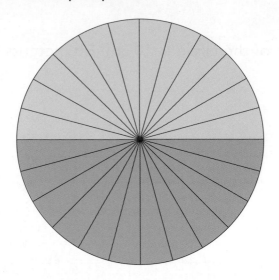

She arranged 23 pieces to form a pattern like this:

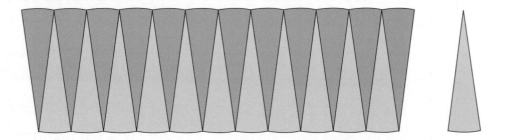

Then she cut the last piece into halves. She placed one half at each end of her pattern to make it look like a rectangle.

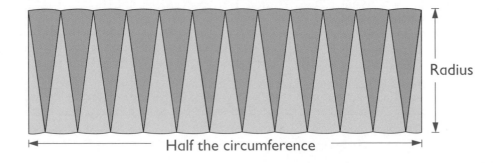

Radius

Half the circumference

Half the circumference
= $\pi \times$ Radius

32

$$\boxed{\text{Area of circle} = \pi \times \text{Radius} \times \text{Radius}}$$

Taking $\pi = 3.14$, find the area of a circle of radius 10 cm.

Area of circle $= \pi \times 10 \times 10$
$= 3.14 \times 10 \times 10$
$= \blacksquare$ cm^2

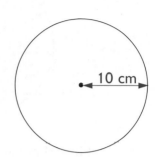

2. The radius of a circle is 14 cm. Find its area. $\left(\text{Take } \pi = \dfrac{22}{7}\right)$

Area of circle $= \pi \times 14 \times 14$

$= \dfrac{22}{7} \times 14 \times 14$

$= \blacksquare$ cm^2

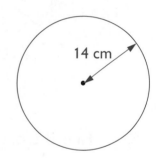

3. The diameter of a circle is 8 cm. Find its area. (Take $\pi = 3.14$)

Radius $= 8 \div 2 = 4$ cm
Area $= \pi \times 4 \times 4$
$= \blacksquare$ cm^2

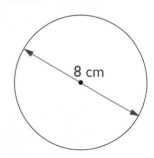

4. Find the area of a circle of radius 7 m. $\left(\text{Take } \pi = \dfrac{22}{7}\right)$

5. Find the area of a circle of diameter 12 m. (Take $\pi = 3.14$)

6. Find the area of each circle. $\left(\text{Take } \pi = \dfrac{22}{7}\right)$

(a)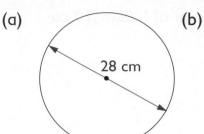
28 cm

(b)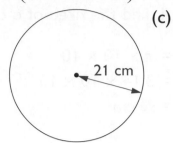
21 cm

(c)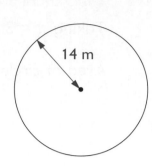
14 m

7. Find the area of each circle. (Take π = 3.14)

(a)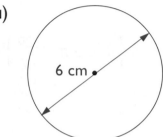
6 cm

(b)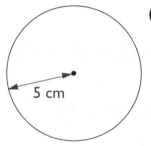
5 cm

(c)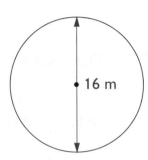
16 m

Workbook Exercise 12

8. Find the area of each semicircular shape. (Take π = 3.14)

(a)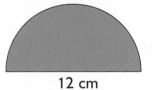
12 cm

(b)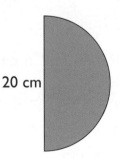
20 cm

9. Each of the following figures is in a shape of a quarter circle. Find its area. (Take π = 3.14)

(a)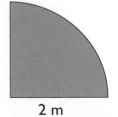
2 m

(b)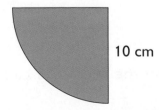
10 cm

Workbook Exercise 13

10. The shaded parts in the following figures are quarter circles. Find the total shaded area in each figure. (Take $\pi = 3.14$)

(a)

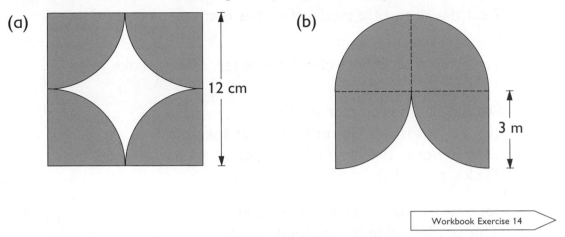

12 cm

(b)

3 m

Workbook Exercise 14

11. The figure is made up of a semicircle, a rectangle and a triangle. Find its area. (Take $\pi = 3.14$)

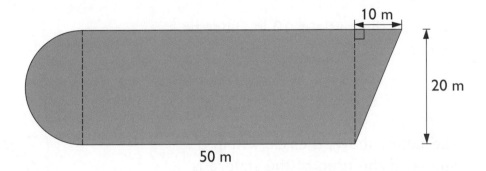

10 m

20 m

50 m

12. The figure shows two semicircles. Find the area of the shaded part in terms of π.

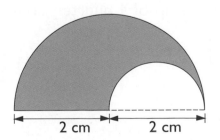

2 cm   2 cm

Workbook Exercises 15 & 16

PRACTICE 2B

1. Find the area of a circle of radius 6 cm. (Take π = 3.14)

2. Find the area of a circle of diameter 28 m. $\left(\text{Take } \pi = \dfrac{22}{7}\right)$

3. A coin has a diameter of 4 cm.
   (a) What is the circumference of the coin?
   (b) What is the area of one face of the coin?
   (Take π = 3.14)

4. John has a semicircular flowerbed.
   The straight side is 2 m long. What
   is the area of the flowerbed?
   (Take π = 3.14)

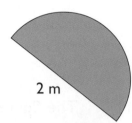

2 m

5. $\dfrac{1}{4}$ of the circle is shaded. If the
   radius of the circle is 10 in., find the
   shaded area. (Take π = 3.14)

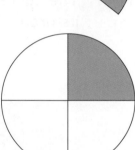

6. The figure shows a circle within a
   square. If the area of the square is
   36 cm², find the area and
   circumference of the circle.
   (Take π = 3.14)

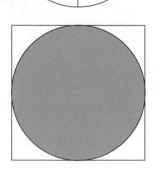

7. The figure is made up of 4 quarter circles. Find its area.
   $\left(\text{Take } \pi = \dfrac{22}{7}\right)$

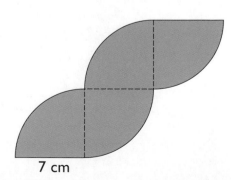

7 cm

PRACTICE 2C

1. A table mat is made up of a square and
   4 semicircles as shown.
   (a) What is the area of the table mat?
   (b) What is its perimeter?

   $\left(\text{Take } \pi = \dfrac{22}{7} \right)$

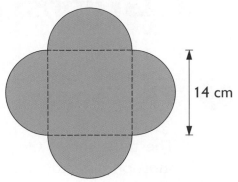

14 cm

2. The figure is made up of a triangle and
   a semicircle. Find its area and perimeter.
   (Take π = 3.14)

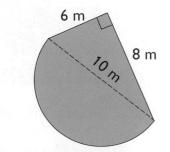

6 m

8 m

10 m

3. The figure shows a square and a
   semicircle. Find the area and perimeter
   of the shaded part. (Take π = 3.14)

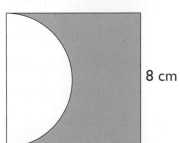

8 cm

4. The figure is made up of two semicircles
   and a quarter circle. Find its area and
   perimeter. Leave your answers in terms
   of π.

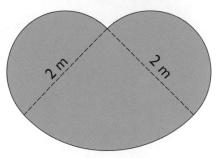

2 m

2 m

5. The figure shows 2 circles. Find the area
   of the shaded part in terms of π.

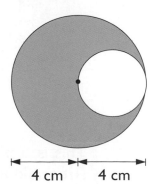

4 cm   4 cm

37

3 Graphs

1 Pie Charts

The table shows the number of T-shirts of different sizes sold in a shop on a certain day.

Size	S	M	L	XL
Number of T-shirts	9	18	6	3

There are 36 T-shirts altogether.

$\frac{1}{4}$ of them are of size S.

What fraction of the T-shirts are of size M?

What fraction of the T-shirts are of size L?

What fraction of the T-shirts are of size XL?

The fractions can be shown like this:

$\frac{9}{36} = \frac{1}{4}$

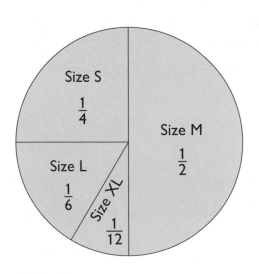

A **pie chart** is a circle graph.

This is a **pie chart**. It represents the number of T-shirts of different sizes sold in the shop.

1.　There are 200 chairs in a warehouse. 80 of them are plastic chairs, 30 are metal chairs, 40 are wicker chairs and the rest are wooden chairs. The pie chart represents the number of chairs of each type.

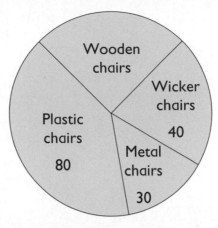

(a)　Which type of chair is found in the greatest quantity?
(b)　How many wooden chairs are there?
(c)　What fraction of the chairs are plastic chairs?
(d)　How many times as many plastic chairs as wicker chairs are there?

2.　The pie chart represents the amount of money collected by various booths at a carnival.

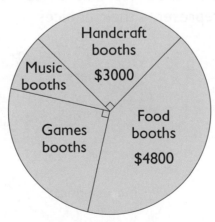

(a)　What fraction of the total amount of money was collected by the games booths?
(b)　What was the total amount of money collected by the various booths?
(c)　How much money was collected by the music booths?
(d)　What was the ratio of the money collected by the food booths to the money collected by the handcraft booths?

Workbook Exercise 17

39

3. A group of 40 boys were asked to choose toast, cereal, pancake or eggs for breakfast on a certain day. The pie chart represents their choices.

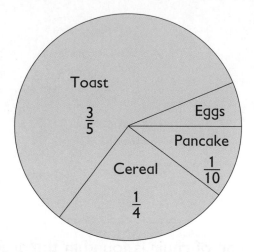

(a) Which type of breakfast did most students have on that day?
(b) What fraction of the students had eggs for breakfast?
(c) How many students had toast for breakfast?
(d) What percentage of the students had cereal for breakfast?

4. The students in a school were asked to name their favorite subject. The pie chart represents their choices.

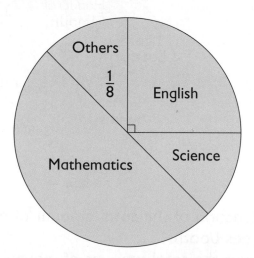

(a) What fraction of the students liked Mathematics?
(b) What percentage of the students liked English?
(c) What fraction of the students liked Science?
(d) If 1200 students liked Mathematics, how many students liked English?

Workbook Exercise 18

5.   A group of 200 students were asked to name their favorite sport.
     The pie chart represents their choices.

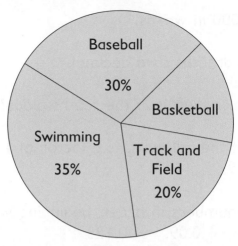

(a)   Which was the most popular sport?
(b)   What percentage of the students chose basketball?
(c)   How many students chose baseball?
(d)   What fraction of the students chose swimming?

6.   Mrs. Gray spent some money on clothes. The pie chart shows how
     the money was spent.

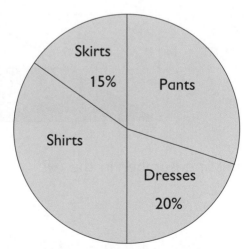

(a)   What did Mrs. Gray spend the most money on?
(b)   What percentage of the money was spent on shirts?
(c)   What percentage of the money was spent on pants?
(d)   If Mrs. Gray spent $60 on pants, how much did she spend
      altogether?

Workbook Exercise 19

REVIEW A

1. Write 2,340,000 in words.

2. Write 57 hundredths as a decimal.

3. In 435.26, which digit is in the tenths place?

4. Which one of the following is a factor of 119?
   3,   7,   9,   11

5. Arrange the numbers in order, beginning with the smallest.
   0.25,   0.5,   0.09,   0.123

6. Which one of the following is 6 kg when rounded off to the nearest kilogram?
   5.49 kg,   5.399 kg,   5.59 kg,   5.499 kg

7. Express 0.125 as a fraction in its simplest form.

8. What fraction of the rectangle is shaded?

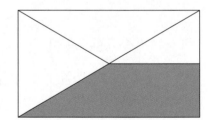

9. What is the missing number in the ■?

   $\frac{12}{5} = ■ + \frac{2}{5}$

10. Find the value of $\frac{2}{9} \div (\frac{4}{9} + \frac{2}{3}) \times \frac{7}{8}$.

11. Find the value of 6.07 × 99.

12. Find the value of 293 ÷ 7 correct to 2 decimal places.

13. Find the value of 15 ÷ 3 + (9 − 6) × 4.

42

14. Which one of the following is the best estimate of the value of 48.59 × 698?

350,   3500,   35,000,   350,000

15. What is the number indicated by the arrow?

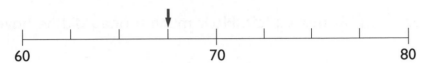

60   70   80

16. (a) Express $1\frac{1}{3}$ hours in minutes.

(b) Express 0.02 kg in grams.

17. How many 250-ml cartons of apple juice must Mrs. Bates buy in order to fill up a jug of capacity 2 liters?

Apple
Juice
250 ml

18. Nicole had 30 boxes of cookies. She sold all of them at 3 boxes for $20. How much money did she receive altogether?

19. A box contained 72 red marbles and blue marbles. There were 20 more red marbles than blue marbles. How many blue marbles were there?

20. An empty basket weighs 0.4 kg. The basket together with 5 mangoes weighs 2 kg. Find the average weight of the mangoes.

21. Sally's weight is 36 kg. Jane is 4 kg heavier than Sally. Find their average weight.

22. The average weight of 3 boys is 35.6 kg. If one of them weighs 34.8 kg, find the average weight of the other two boys.

23. David spent $\frac{2}{5}$ of his money on food and $\frac{1}{4}$ of it on transport. What fraction of his money did he have left?

24. In a class, $\frac{1}{3}$ of the students are girls. $\frac{1}{2}$ of the boys and $\frac{1}{3}$ of the girls can swim. What fraction of the students in the class can swim?

25. Matthew spent $\frac{1}{8}$ of his money on a book and $50 on a radio. He had $\frac{1}{4}$ of his money left. How much money did he have left?

26. The ratio of the number of boys to the number of girls at a fire drill is 3 : 4. If there are 270 boys, how many girls are there?

27. There are 36 children in a dance class. The ratio of the number of boys to the number of girls is 5 : 4. How many more boys than girls are there?

28. $\frac{3}{4}$ of Peter's stamps are U.S. stamps. The rest are Canadian stamps. What percentage of his stamps are Canadian stamps?

29. The price of a bicycle has increased from $200 to $250. By what percentage did the price increase?

30. The usual price of a tennis racket is $40. It is sold at a discount of 30%. Find the selling price.

31. Cameron is driving at a speed of 60 km/h. How far will he travel in 2 hours?

32. The rental rates for a ski chalet are as follows:

Weekdays	$50 per day
Saturdays & Sundays	$70 per day

Mr. Bell and his family stayed at the chalet from Thursday to Sunday. How much did they have to pay?

33. At a sale, Peter bought 4 books and John bought 7 books. John paid $1.95 more than Peter. If all the books were of the same price, how much did they pay altogether?

34. Mary spent $300 of her monthly salary on rent. She spent $\frac{1}{2}$ of the remainder on food and $120 on transport. If she had $160 left, find her monthly salary.

35. $\frac{3}{4}$ of a sum of money is $1800. How much is $\frac{2}{5}$ of the sum of money?

36. Tyrone has 3 times as much money as Ryan. If Tyrone's money is halved and Ryan's money is doubled, what will be the ratio of Tyrone's money to Ryan's money?

37. Each month, Emily spends 70% of her salary. She gives 40% of the remainder to charity and saves the rest. If she saves $360, how much is her monthly salary?

38. Joe, John and Peter shared a sum of money. Joe received 40% of the money. The ratio of John's share to Peter's share was 1 : 3. If Peter received $90 more than John, how much money did Joe receive?

39. John took 4 hours to cycle $\frac{3}{5}$ of a trip. He took 2 hours to cycle the remaining 30 km. Find his average speed for the whole trip.

40. If $p = 3$, find the value of

    (a) $\dfrac{10 - p}{p}$

    (b) $5p^2 - 9$

41. The average weight of 3 boxes is x kg. If one of them weighs 2 kg, find the average weight of the other two boxes in terms of x.

42. A square has the same perimeter as the triangle.
Find the area of the square.

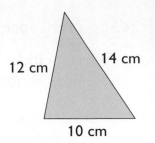

12 cm

14 cm

10 cm

43. The figure is made up of a square and a semicircle.
Find its perimeter. (Take π = 3.14)

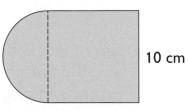

10 cm

44. Each of the following figures is made up of 6 squares. Which figure
does not have a line of symmetry?

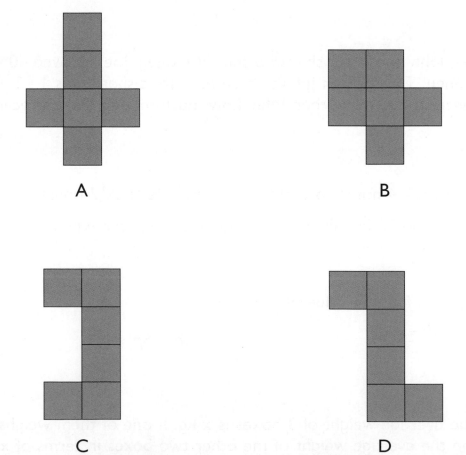

A

B

C

D

45. Copy the shape on dotted paper. Then use the shape to make a tessellation.

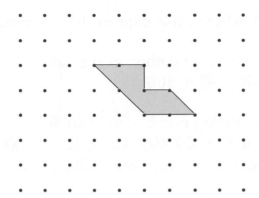

46. The bar graph shows the daily attendance of a class of 40 students.

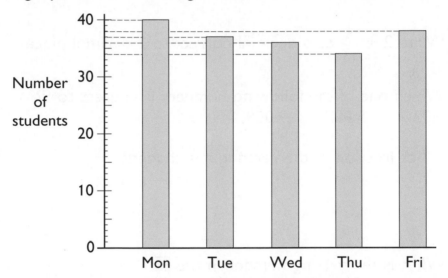

(a) On which day was the attendance the lowest?

(b) What percentage of the students were absent on Friday?

(c) What was the average daily attendance?

47. A group of students were asked to name their favorite activity in school. The pie chart represents their choices.

(a) What percentage of the students liked the school band?

(b) What fraction of the students liked swimming?

(c) If 18 students liked the art club, find the total number of students in the group.

REVIEW B

1. In 6,543,000, what is the digit in the ten thousands place?

2. What is the missing number in the ■?
   $630,508 = 630 \times$ ■ $+ 508$

3. What is the missing number in each ■?
   (a) The digit 3 in 837,405 stands for $3 \times$ ■.
   (b) The value of the digit 6 in 2.067 is ■.

4. Which one of the following has 4 as a factor?
   27,   36,   58,   62

5. Write $2 + \dfrac{8}{15}$ as a decimal correct to 2 decimal places.

6. Which one of the following numbers is nearest to 9?
   9.03,   9.09,   9.009,   9.1

7. What fraction of the rectangle is shaded?

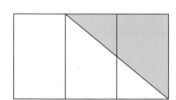

8. What is the missing number in the ■?

   $3.004 = 3 + \dfrac{4}{■}$

9. Express each of the following as a fraction in its simplest form.
   (a) 0.048   (b) 36%

10. Arrange the fractions in order, beginning with the smallest.
    $\dfrac{62}{100}$, $\dfrac{31}{20}$, $\dfrac{3}{5}$, $\dfrac{12}{25}$

11. Find the value of each of the following:
    (a) $64 - (24 - 18) \times 10$ (b) $\dfrac{3}{10} + \dfrac{1}{6} \div (\dfrac{5}{6} - \dfrac{4}{5})$

12. What is the missing number in the ■?
    $6.5 \div$ ■ $= 0.065$

13.   A shop is open from 10:15 a.m. to 9:30 p.m. How long is the shop open?

14. $\frac{3}{4}$ liter of milk can fill 4 glasses. How many glasses can 3 liters of milk fill?

15.   Brenda had 1 kg 300 g of mushrooms. She used 450 g for cooking soup. How much mushrooms did she have left?

16.   At a fruit stand, oranges are sold at 5 for $2. How many oranges can Mrs. King buy with $24?

17.   At a department store, a gift certificate is given for every $40 spent. If Sandy buys an oven which costs $350, how many gift certificates will she get?

18.   Vince sent some postcards to Canada. The postage for each postcard was 30¢. If he spent a total of $4.80 on postage, how many postcards did he send?

19.   The average of three numbers is 45. If the average of two of the numbers is 47, what is the third number?

20.   Water flows from a tap into an empty tank at the rate of 8 gal per minute. How long will it take to fill up the tank if its capacity is 200 gal?

21.   Susan bought $\frac{1}{2}$ of a pizza. She ate $\frac{2}{3}$ of the pizza she bought. What fraction of a whole pizza did she have left?

22.   Andrew spent $\frac{1}{4}$ of his money on a book and $\frac{1}{2}$ of the remainder on a photo album. What fraction of his money did he spend altogether?

23.   Find the missing number in each ■.
       (a)   3 : 8 = ■ : 32   (b)   2 : 5 : ■ = 14 : 35 : 49

24.   A rope 60 yd long is cut into three pieces in the ratio 3 : 2 : 7. What is the length of the longest piece?

25. The number of students in a school has increased from 2500 to 2800. By what percentage did the number increase?

26. Peter has 600 Singapore stamps and 200 other stamps. What percentage of his stamps are Singapore stamps?

27. Find the value of 15% of $30.

28. Juan took 40 seconds to swim 50 m. Find his average speed in m/s.

29. Jack had 130 stickers and Kara had 50 stickers. After Jack gave Kara some stickers, Jack had twice as many stickers as Kara. How many stickers did Jack give Kara?

30. Bruce bought 100 greeting cards for $60. He sold $\frac{3}{5}$ of them at 3 for $2. He sold the rest at 75¢ each. How much money did he make?

31. $\frac{1}{3}$ of the beads in a box are red, $\frac{2}{3}$ of the remainder are blue and the rest are yellow. If there are 24 red beads, how many yellow beads are there?

32. In a school band, $\frac{1}{2}$ of the members were boys. At the end of the year, 8 girls left the band and the ratio of the number of boys to the number of girls was 4 : 3. How many girls remained in the band?

33. The ratio of John's weight to Peter's weight is 5 : 3. Their average weight is 40 lb. Find John's weight.

34. Mary's savings is $\frac{3}{5}$ of Susan's savings. If Susan saves $60 more than Mary, how much money do they save altogether?

35. In a class, 60% of the students are boys. 10% of the boys and 30% of the girls walk to school. What percentage of the students in the class walk to school?

36. John saved $75 in January and $60 in February. How many percent more did he save in January than in February?

37. Terry drove for 40 minutes at an average speed of 90 km/h. Then he drove for 20 minutes to complete the remaining 25 km. Find his average speed for the whole trip.

38. The figure is made up of a rectangle and a triangle. The area of the rectangle is 72 in.². Find the area of the triangle.

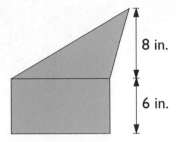

8 in.

6 in.

39. A quarter circle is cut off from a triangle as shown. Find the area of the remaining figure. $\left(\text{Take } \pi = \frac{22}{7} \right)$

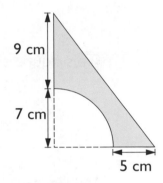

9 cm

7 cm

5 cm

40. The figure shows two quarter circles within a square. Find the perimeter of the shaded part. (Take π = 3.14)

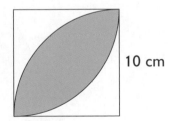

10 cm

41. Copy the symmetric figure on a square grid. Then draw a line of symmetry of the figure.

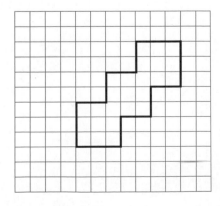

42. The figure shows a solid that is made up of unit cubes. At least how many unit cubes are needed to add onto the solid to complete a cuboid?

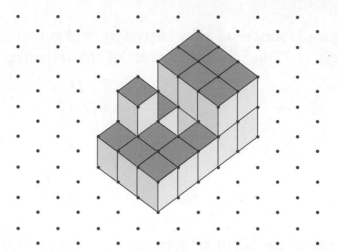

43. This figure shows a solid.

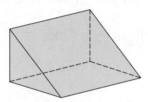

Which one of the following is a net of the solid?

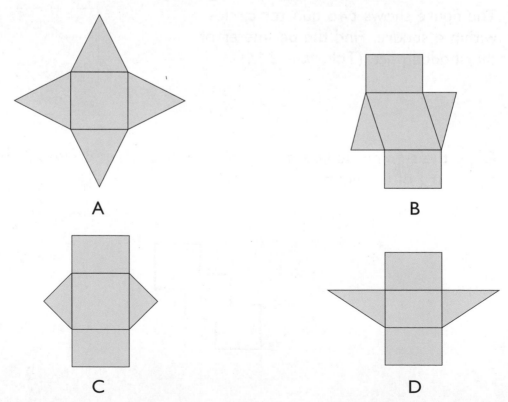

A   B

C   D

44. A group of students were asked to choose an after school activity they would like to join. The pie chart represents their choices.

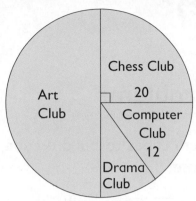

(a) How many students chose the Art Club?
(b) What percentage of the students chose the Chess Club?
(c) How many students chose the Drama Club?
(d) How many students were there in the group?

45. The line graph shows the sales of T-shirts over 5 months.

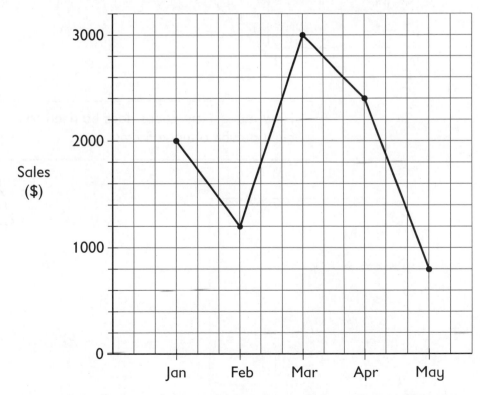

(a) What was the increase in sales from February to March?
(b) What was the average monthly sales?
(c) If each T-shirt was sold for $4 in April, how many T-shirts were sold that month?

4 Volume

1 Solving Problems

Mingde uses 1-cm cubes to build a cube of edge 4 cm. How many cubes does he use?

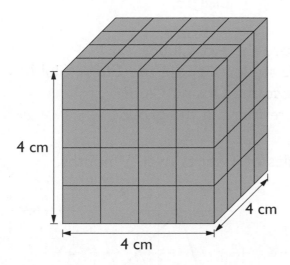

$4 \times 4 \times 4$

How many 1-cm cubes does he need to build a cube of edge 5 cm?

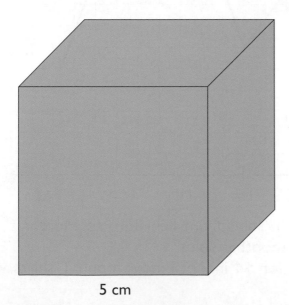

5 cm

If he builds a cube with 729 pieces of 1-cm cubes, find the edge of the cube.

1. The figure shows a solid consisting of 10 cubes of edge 2 cm. Find its volume.

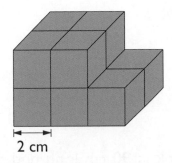

2 cm

2. How many cubes of edge 2 cm are needed to build a cuboid measuring 10 cm by 10 cm by 6 cm?

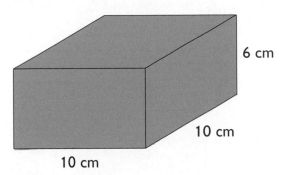

6 cm

10 cm

10 cm

3. The base of a cuboid measures 20 cm by 12 cm. If the volume of the cuboid is 3600 cm³, find its height.

Height = $\dfrac{3600}{20 \times 12}$

= ■ cm

$20 \times 12 \times$ Height = 3600

Workbook Exercise 20

4. A rectangular container measuring 20 cm by 20 cm by 22 cm is $\frac{1}{2}$ filled with oil. Find the volume of the oil in liters.
(1 liter = 1000 cm³)

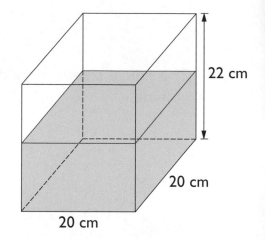

Height of oil level = 22 ÷ 2
                    = 11 cm

Volume of oil = 20 × 20 × 11
             = 4400 cm³
             = ■ ℓ

5. A rectangular tank is 90 cm long and 50 cm wide. It contains 162 liters of water when it is $\frac{2}{3}$ full. Find the height of the tank.
(1 liter = 1000 cm³)

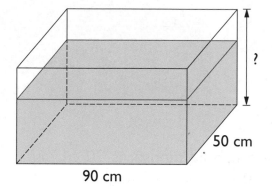

Volume of water = 162 ℓ
               = 162 × 1000 cm³

Height of water level = $\frac{162 \times 1000}{90 \times 50}$
                      = ■ cm

Height of the tank = ■ cm

Workbook Exercise 21

6. A rectangular tank, 35 cm long and 25 cm wide, contained some water and a stone. The height of the water level was 10 cm. When the stone was taken out, the water level dropped to 8 cm. Find the volume of the stone.

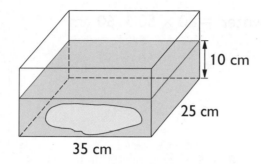

Decrease in height of water level = 10 − 8 = 2 cm

Volume of the stone = 35 × 25 × 2 = ■ cm³

7. A rectangular tank measuring 50 cm by 40 cm by 40 cm is $\frac{1}{2}$ filled with water. When 3 metal cubes of edge 10 cm are placed in the tank, the water level rises. Find the height of the new water level.

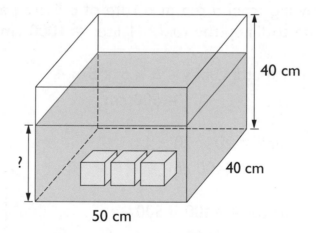

Volume of 3 metal cubes = 10 × 10 × 10 × 3 = 3000 cm³

Increase in height of water level = $\dfrac{3000}{50 \times 40}$ = ■ cm

Height of the new water level = ■ cm

Workbook Exercise 22

8. A rectangular tank measures 80 cm by 50 cm by 60 cm. It is filled with water to its brim. If the water is drained out at a rate of 12 liters per minute, how long will it take to empty the tank? (1 liter = 1000 cm³)

Volume of water = 80 × 50 × 60 cm³

$$= \frac{80 \times 50 \times 60}{1000} \ell$$

$$= 8 \times 5 \times 6 \ \ell$$

Time taken $= \dfrac{8 \times 5 \times 6}{12}$

= ■ min

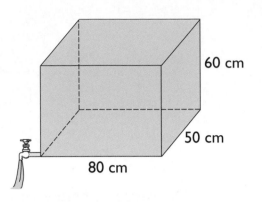

60 cm
50 cm
80 cm

9. 4 metal cubes of edge 5 cm are placed in an empty rectangular tank measuring 20 cm by 20 cm by 11 cm. The tank is then filled with water flowing from a tap at a rate of 6 liters per minute. How long will it take to fill up the tank? (1 liter = 1000 cm³)

Volume of 4 metal cubes = 5 × 5 × 5 × 4
= 500 cm³

Volume of tank = 20 × 20 × 11
= 4400 cm³

Volume of water = 4400 − 500
= 3900 cm³
= 3.9 ℓ

Time taken $= \dfrac{3.9}{6}$

= ■ min

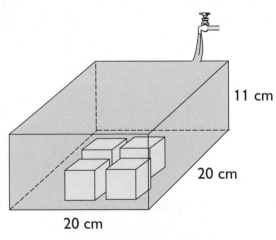

11 cm
20 cm
20 cm

Workbook Exercise 23

PRACTICE 4A

1. The volume of a cube is 216 cm³. Find the area of one face of the cube.

2. The volume of a box is 3600 cm³. Its width is 15 cm. Its length is twice its width. Find its height.

3. Find the unknown edge of each cuboid.

(a)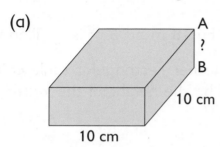

A
?
B

10 cm

10 cm

Volume = 400 cm³
AB = ■ cm

(b)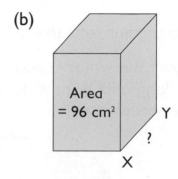

Area
= 96 cm²

Y

?

X

Volume = 768 cm³
XY = ■ cm

4. The figure shows a cuboid consisting of 12 cubes.
   The area of the shaded face is 36 cm².
   (a) Find the volume of each cube.
   (b) Find the volume of the cuboid.

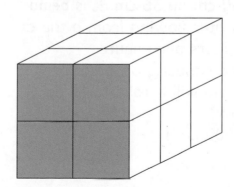

5. The figure shows a solid that is made up of
   4 cubes of edge 2 cm.
   (a) Find the volume of the solid.
   (b) If the solid is painted red, find the total area
       which is painted red.

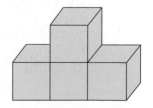

59

PRACTICE 4B

1. The base of a rectangular tank measures 50 cm by 40 cm. What will be the height of the water level when it contains 9 liters of water?
(1 liter = 1000 cm³)

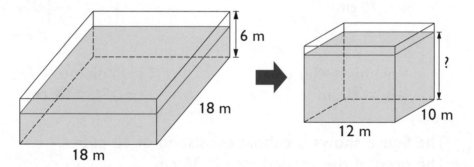

2. A rectangular tank measuring 18 m by 18 m by 6 m is $\frac{2}{3}$ filled with water. If the water is poured into another rectangular tank which is 12 m long and 10 m wide, what will be the height of the water level in the second tank?

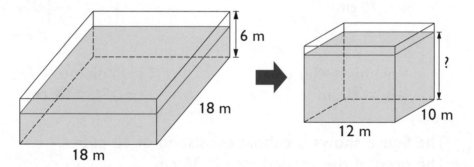

3. An empty rectangular tank measures 60 cm by 50 cm by 56 cm. It is being filled with water flowing from a tap at a rate of 8 liters per minute.
   (a) Find the capacity of the tank.
   (b) How long will it take to fill up the tank?
   (1 liter = 1000 cm³)

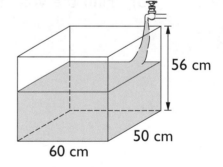

4. The base of a rectangular tank measures 50 cm by 40 cm. It contains 60 liters of water when it is $\frac{3}{4}$ full. Find the height of the tank. (1 liter = 1000 cm³)

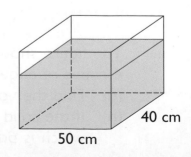

PRACTICE 4C

1. A rectangular tank, 25 cm long and 25 cm wide, is filled with water to a depth of 10 cm. When a metal cube of edge 10 cm is placed in the tank, the water level rises. Find the height of the new water level.

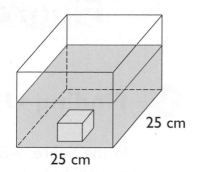

2. A rectangular tank measuring 50 cm by 50 cm by 42 cm was $\frac{2}{3}$ filled with water. When a stone was placed in the tank, the tank became $\frac{3}{4}$ full.

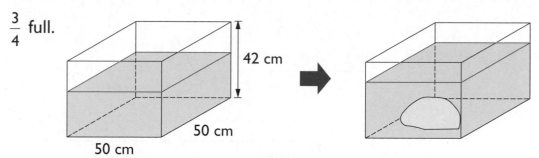

   (a) Find the capacity of the tank in cubic centimeters.
   (b) Find the volume of the stone.

3. An empty rectangular tank measures 70 cm by 25 cm by 36 cm. A stone of volume 4500 cm³ is placed in the tank. Then the tank is filled with water flowing from a tap at a rate of 9 liters per minute. How long will it take to fill up the tank?
   (1 liter = 1000 cm³)

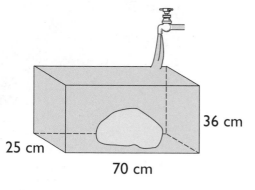

*4. Ben placed a stone in an empty rectangular tank, 50 cm long and 40 cm wide. He then filled the tank with water flowing from a tap at a rate of 10 liters per minute. It took 3 minutes to fill the tank to a depth of 18 cm to cover the stone completely. Find the volume of the stone.
   (1 liter = 1000 cm³)

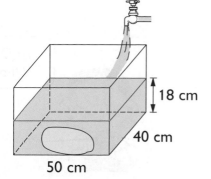

61

5 Triangles and 4-sided Figures

① Finding Unknown Angles

In the figure, ABCE is a parallelogram, CDE is an equilateral triangle and BCD is a straight line.

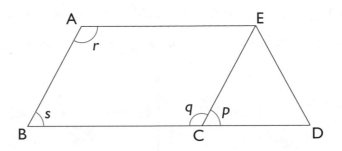

$\angle p = \blacksquare °$

$\angle q = \blacksquare °$

$\angle r = \blacksquare °$

$\angle s = \blacksquare °$

CDE is an equilateral triangle.
What can you say about its angles?

ABCE is a parallelogram.
What can you say about its angles?

ABDE is a trapezoid.
What can you say about its angles?

1. In the figure, XW = XY, ∠WXY = 38° and XYZ is a straight line. Find ∠XWY and ∠WYZ.

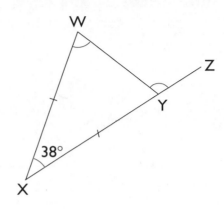

∠XWY = (180° − 38°) ÷ 2

= ■°

∠WYZ = ■°

2. In trapezoid ABCD, AD // BC, ∠ABC = 82° and ∠ADC = 48°. Find ∠BAD and ∠BCD.

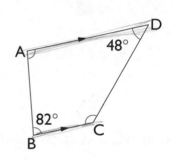

Each pair of angles between two parallel sides add up to 180°.

∠BAD = 180° − 82° = ■°

∠BCD = 180° − 48° = ■°

3. In rhombus WXYZ, ∠WXY = 84°. Find ∠WZY and ∠XWY.

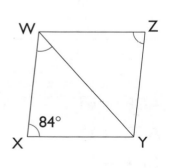

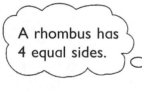

A rhombus has 4 equal sides.

∠WZY = ■°

∠XWY = ■°

Workbook Exercise 24

4. In the figure, WXYZ is a parallelogram, ZV = ZW, ∠ZVW = 52° and VWX is a straight line. Find ∠XYZ.

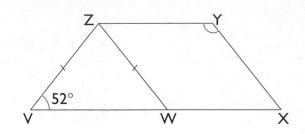

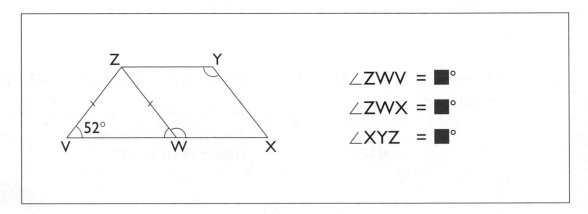

∠ZWV = ■°
∠ZWX = ■°
∠XYZ = ■°

5. In the figure, ABCE is a square, AC = CD and BCD is a straight line. Find ∠ACE and ∠CDA.

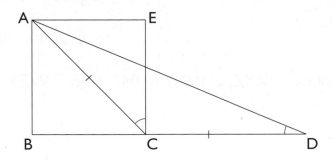

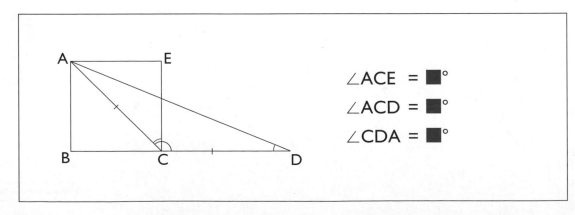

∠ACE = ■°
∠ACD = ■°
∠CDA = ■°

6. In the figure, PQRT is a parallelogram, QR = RS, ∠TRS = 90° and ∠QPT = 62°. Find ∠RSQ.

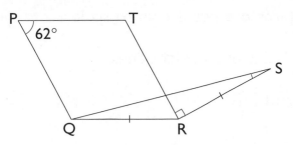

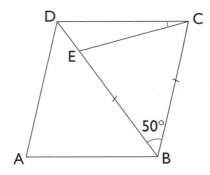

∠QRT = ■°

∠QRS = ■°

∠RSQ = ■°

7. In the figure, ABCD is a rhombus, BE = BC and ∠CBE = 50°. Find ∠DCE.

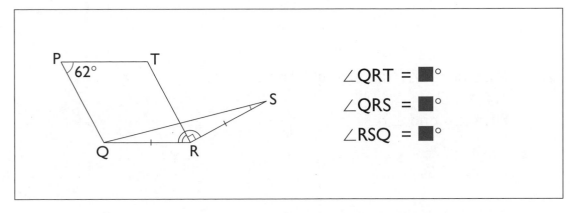

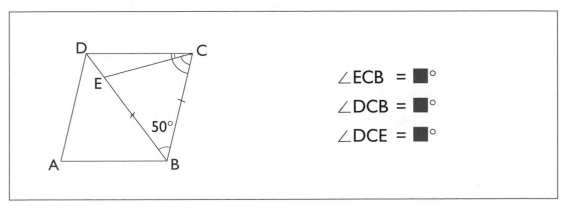

∠ECB = ■°

∠DCB = ■°

∠DCE = ■°

Workbook Exercise 25

PRACTICE 5A

The following figures are not drawn to scale.

1. XPY and XQZ are straight lines.
   PQ // YZ
   Find ∠a and ∠b.

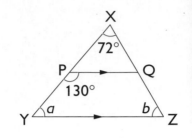

2. XZS and YZT are straight lines.
   XY = XZ
   Find ∠p and ∠q.

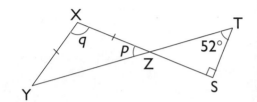

3. ABC is a right-angled triangle.
   BCD is an isosceles triangle.
   BC = BD
   Find ∠x.

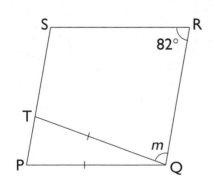

4. PQRS is a parallelogram.
   PQ = TQ
   Find ∠m.

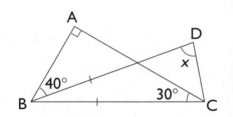

5. EFGH is a parallelogram.
   FG = FH
   Find ∠h.

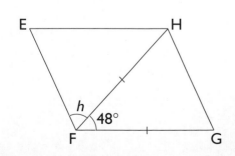

PRACTICE 5B

The following figures are not drawn to scale.

1. MKL is an equilateral triangle.
    IM // JL
    Find ∠p and ∠q.

    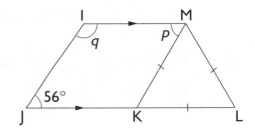

2. ABCD is a parallelogram.
    CDE is a straight line.
    Find ∠a and ∠b.

    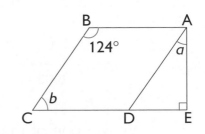

3. UWX and VWZ are straight lines.
    VW = UW
    WZ // XY
    Find ∠x and ∠y.

    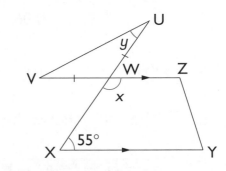

4. FGHI is a rectangle.
    IJHK is a rhombus.
    Find ∠m.

    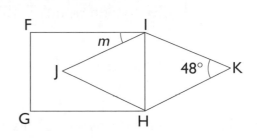

5. PQRS is a square.
    RST is an isosceles triangle.
    RS = ST
    Find ∠w.

    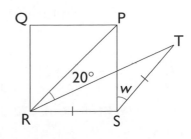

REVIEW C

1. Write the following in figures.
   (a) Thirty thousand, thirty
   (b) Three million, forty thousand

2. What is the missing number in each ■?
   (a) 6205 = 6 × 1000 + 2 × ■ + 5
   (b) 2.098 = 2 + ■ + 0.008

3. What is the number indicated by the arrow?

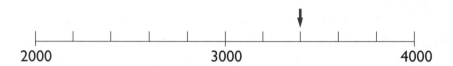

4. Which one of the following is the best estimate of the value of 3594 ÷ 597?
   6,   0.6,   0.06,   0.006

5. Write 100 ÷ 3 as a mixed number.

6. The table shows the rates of charges for printing T-shirts.

   | First 50 T-shirts | $9 each |
   | Every additional T-shirt | $8 |

   George printed 80 T-shirts. How much did he have to pay?

7. Norman gave $\frac{1}{3}$ of his money to his wife. He divided the remainder equally between his 3 children. What fraction of his money did each of his children receive?

8. A container is $\frac{2}{3}$ full when it contains 60 gal of water. How much water is in the container when it is $\frac{3}{5}$ full?

68

9. Find the value of each of the following:

   (a) $\dfrac{3}{4} + \dfrac{1}{12} \times 4 \div \dfrac{2}{3}$

   (b) $6 \div \dfrac{3}{5} + \dfrac{2}{5} \times \dfrac{5}{6}$

10. $\dfrac{1}{3}$ of John's savings is twice as much as David's savings. Find the ratio of John's savings to David's savings.

11. The ratio of John's money to Peter's money is 3 : 5. Express Peter's money as a fraction of John's money.

12. John spent $32 and had $48 left. What percentage of his money did he spend?

13. $\dfrac{1}{4}$ of a circle is colored blue. 20% of the remainder is colored red. What percentage of the circle is colored red?

14. The pie chart shows how a group of students travel to school.
    What percentage of the students walk to school?

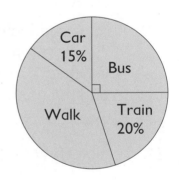

15. Express 2.5% as a fraction in its simplest form.

16. Find the value of 20% of $14.50.

17. Ronald started jogging at 6:30 a.m. By 8:30 a.m., he had jogged a distance of 8 km. Find his average speed in km/h.

18. Marcus earns 3¢ from every newspaper he delivers. He earns an extra $3 for every 400 newspapers delivered. How much will he earn if he delivers 2000 newspapers?

19. A tank was $\dfrac{2}{5}$ filled with water. After another 36 liters of water were poured in, the tank became $\dfrac{2}{3}$ full. Find the capacity of the tank.

20. The ratio of the number of blue beads to the number of red beads in a jar was 2 : 5 at first. Ian removed $\frac{1}{4}$ of the blue beads and $\frac{2}{5}$ of the red beads from the jar.
    (a) Find the new ratio of the number of blue beads to the number of red beads.
    (b) If there were 12 more red beads than blue beads left in the jar, how many beads were removed altogether?

21. The width of a rectangle is $\frac{2}{3}$ of its length. If the perimeter of the rectangle is 40 cm, find the area of the rectangle.

22. Tyrone took $1\frac{1}{2}$ hours to cover $\frac{2}{3}$ of a trip. He took $\frac{1}{2}$ hour to cover the remaining trip at an average speed of 72 km/h. Find his average speed for the whole trip.

23. John and David both drove a distance of 80 km from Town X to Town Y. John left Town X 20 minutes earlier than David. They reached Town Y at the same time. If John's average speed was 60 km/h, find David's average speed.

24. Simplify $9t - 6t + t - 2$.

25. Elaine bought 3 bottles of shampoo at $\$n$ each and 5 tubes of toothpaste at \$2 each. She gave the cashier \$50. How much change did she receive? Give your answer in terms of n.

26. In the figure, not drawn to scale, find $\angle x$.

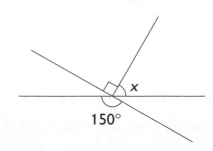

150°

70

27. In the figure, not drawn to scale, PQ = PR = RS. QRS is a straight line. Find ∠RPS.

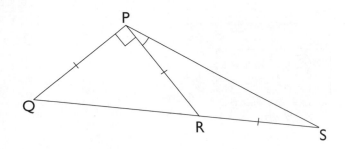

28. In the figure, ABCD is a parallelogram. Find ∠x.

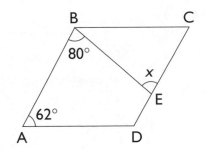

29. Find the shaded area in the rectangle.

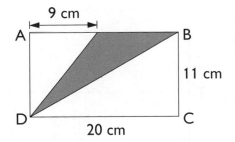

30. The figure shows three semicircular shapes of the same size. Find its area in terms of π.

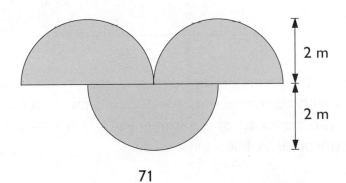

31. Cuboid A has the same volume as Cuboid B. Find the height of Cuboid B.

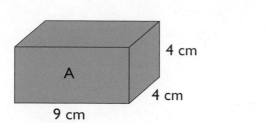 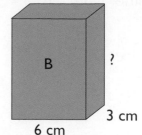

32. A rectangular tank, measuring 40 cm by 30 cm by 30 cm, is $\frac{1}{2}$ filled with water. If the water is drained out at a rate of 10 liters per minute, how long will it take to empty the water from the tank? (1 liter = 1000 cm³)

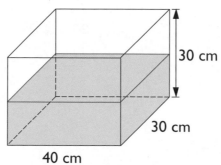

33. The bar graph shows the amounts of water in 5 containers, A, B, C, D and E.

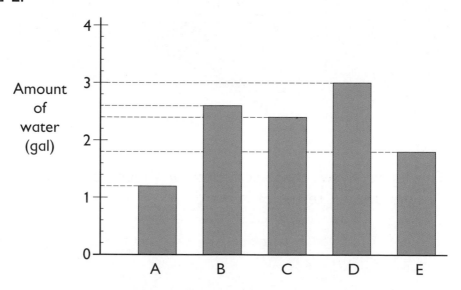

    (a) Find the average amount of water in each container.
    (b) Which container has twice as much water as Container A?
    (c) If the capacity of Container C is 4 gal, what fraction of the container is filled with water?

REVIEW D

1. What is the missing number in each ■?
    (a) $80,609 = 80,000 +$ ■ $+ 9$
    (b) $6.708 = 6 + \dfrac{7}{10} + \dfrac{8}{■}$

2. Find the value of each of the following:
    (a) $(84 - 4 \times 15) \div 3$ (b) $7 \times 8 - 42 \div 7$

3. Find the value of $478 \div 36$ correct to 2 decimal places.

4. Express each of the following as a decimal.
    (a) $\dfrac{3}{8}$ (b) 82%

5. Which one of the following fractions is the smallest?
    $$\dfrac{3}{15}, \qquad \dfrac{3}{7}, \qquad \dfrac{3}{4}, \qquad \dfrac{2}{5}$$

6. Find the value of $\dfrac{1}{3} \times 4.2$.

7. A bus took 4 hours and 35 minutes to travel from Town A to Town B. It reached Town B at 2:00 p.m. What time did it leave Town A?

8. Express each of the following as a fraction in its simplest form.
    (a) 8%   (b) 4.28

9. Express each of the following as a percentage.
    (a) $\dfrac{8}{25}$ (b) 0.45

10. What fraction of 2 kg is 275 g? Give your answer in its simplest form.

11. Find the value of $4 \div \dfrac{7}{8} \times (\dfrac{1}{6} + \dfrac{1}{8})$.

12. What is the missing number in each ■?
    (a) $\dfrac{5}{8} =$ ■ $: 8$ (b) $2 : 3 : 5 =$ ■ $: 9 :$ ■

13. Scott bought 15 oranges at 3 for $1. How much did he pay?

14. Jim and David have $603 altogether. Jim has $115 more than David. How much money does David have?

15. There are 144 people in a hall. 56 of them are women. The rest are men. What fraction of the people in the hall are men?

16. Annie and Betty shared $\frac{1}{2}$ of a pizza. Betty received twice as much as Annie. What fraction of a whole pizza did Betty receive?

17. Heather bought $\frac{1}{2}$ kg of shrimps at $0.90 per 100 g. How much did she pay?

18. Alicia spent 15% of her money on a music box. If the music box cost $60, how much did she have left?

19. During a sale, a shop reduced the prices of all its watches by 30%.
    (a) If the usual price of a watch was $55, find its sale price.
    (b) If the sale price of a watch was $42, find its usual price.

20. Pablo is cycling at a speed of 200 m/min. How long will he take to cycle 1 km?

21. Russell had 240 apples and pears. After selling 82 apples and 26 pears, he had 3 times as many apples as pears left. How many apples did he have at first?

22. Alan, Dave and Linda shared 600 stamps. Dave received twice as many stamps as Alan. Linda received 40 more stamps than Alan. How many stamps did Alan receive?

23. John and Mary had $350 altogether. After John spent $\frac{1}{2}$ of his money and Mary spent $\frac{1}{3}$ of her money, they each had an equal amount of money left. How much did they spend altogether?

24. Mrs. Hall had 84 tarts. 24 of them were cherry tarts. The rest were pineapple tarts and apple tarts. There were 18 more pineapple tarts than cherry tarts. Find the ratio of the number of pineapple tarts to the number of cherry tarts to the number of apple tarts.

25. Jessica had goldfish and angelfish for sale. She sold $\frac{3}{4}$ of the goldfish and $\frac{1}{2}$ of the angelfish. If she had 20 goldfish and 30 angelfish left, how many fish did Jessica have altogether at first?

26. The ratio of Tom's money to Jake's money to Harry's money is 3 : 2 : 4. If Jake gives $\frac{1}{4}$ of his money to Harry, what will be the new ratio of Tom's money to Jake's money to Harry's money?

27. The ratio of Dan's money to Jason's money was 3 : 2. After Dan gave Jason $15, Dan still had $10 more than Jason. How much money did Dan have at first?

28. Mrs. Hoff used 40% of a bag of flour to bake cakes. She used 35% of the remainder to make pizzas. What percentage of the bag of flour did she use to make pizzas?

29. Steve and Jimmy cycled from Town A to Town B at 15 km/h and 12 km/h respectively. They both started from Town A at 10:00 a.m. If Jimmy reached Town B at 10:30 a.m., what time did Steve reach Town B?

30. Peter and David start out on a 10-km walk at the same time. When Peter completes the 10 km, David still has 2 km to walk. If Peter's walking speed is 5 km/h, find David's walking speed.

31. Simplify $4a + 6 + 8a - 3 - a$.

32. The figure is made up of a semicircle, a square and a triangle. Find its area. (Take $\pi = 3.14$)

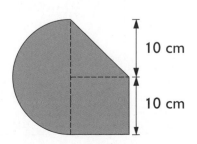

10 cm

10 cm

75

33. Tank A has a square base of area 36 cm² and its height is 8 cm. It is completely filled with water. Tank B is empty and it measures 5 cm by 3 cm by 12 cm. The water in Tank A is poured into Tank B to fill it to its brim. Find the height of the new water level in Tank A.

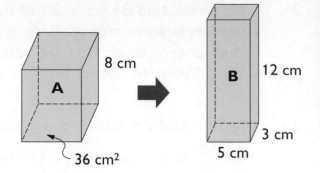

34. In the figure, not drawn to scale, ACE and BCD are straight lines. Find ∠CDE.

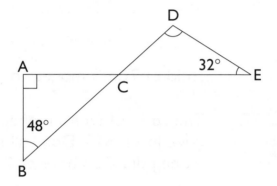

35. Which solid can be formed by the given net?

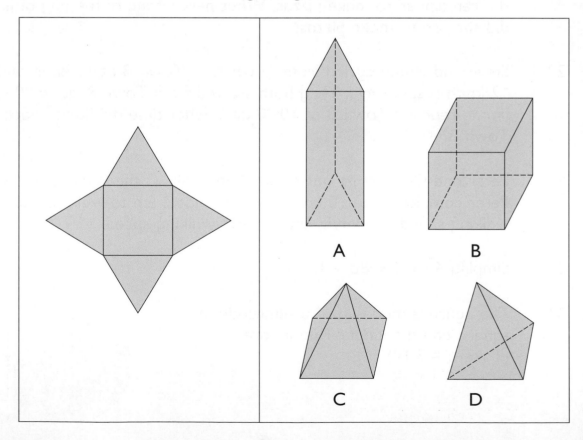

A

B

C

D

36. The figure shows half of a symmetric figure which has the dotted line as a line of symmetry. Copy and complete the symmetric figure on dotted paper.

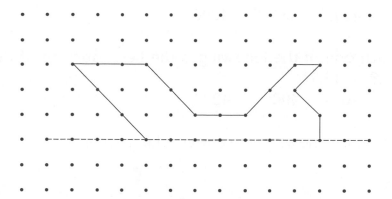

37. The line graph shows the amount of gas used by Justin in the first 6 months of a year.

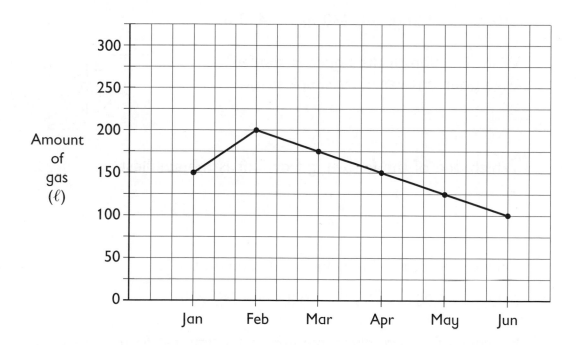

(a) What was the increase in the amount of gas used from January to February?

(b) What was the average amount of gas used per month?

(c) If gas cost $1.15 per liter, how much did Justin spend on gas in February?

REVIEW E

1. Find the value of 2400 ÷ 3000.

2. Find the value of 6.5 × 4000.

3. Which one of the following is the best estimate of the value of 796.8 ÷ 19.2?
   4,   40,   400,   4000

4. The figure shows part of a weighing scale.

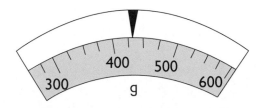

   Which one of the following is closest to the reading indicated by the arrow?
   410 g,   420 g,   430 g,   450 g

5. What fraction of the figure is shaded?
   Give your answer in its simplest form.

6. Which one of the following fractions is the smallest?

   $\dfrac{5}{3}$, $\dfrac{4}{5}$, $\dfrac{9}{10}$, $1\dfrac{1}{2}$

7. Which one of the following is the same as $\dfrac{2}{25}$?

   0.02,   0.08,   0.2,   0.8

8. Express 2.08 as a mixed number in its simplest form.

9. Arrange the lengths in increasing order.

   2 m,   2.6 m,   2.49 m, $2\dfrac{1}{4}$ m

10. Express 45 minutes out of 2 hours as a fraction in its simplest form.

11. The capacity of a cup is $\frac{1}{4}$ qt. How many cups of water will make up 2 qt?

12. Sonya had 45 oranges. She sold all of them at 3 for $2. How much money did she receive?

13. Mary bought 3 kg of shrimps and 3 kg of beef. She spent a total of $46.50. If 1 kg of shrimps cost $9, find the cost of 1 kg of beef.

14. Dorothy can type 225 words in 5 minutes. At this rate, if she types from 10:30 a.m. to 11:15 a.m., how many words will she type?

15. If $\frac{2}{3}$ of a number is 12, what is the value of $\frac{1}{2}$ of the number?

16. Claire bought some cupcakes. She put $\frac{2}{5}$ of them on a tray and the rest in a box. If there were 8 cupcakes on the tray, how many cupcakes were there in the box?

17. 10 glasses of water can fill $\frac{5}{8}$ of a bottle. How many **more** glasses of water are needed to fill up the bottle?

18. There are 40 children in a class. 24 of them are boys. What is the ratio of the number of boys to the number of girls?

19. The average weight of a man and a boy is 60 kg. If the boy weighs $\frac{2}{3}$ as much as the man, what is the weight of the boy?

20. Jean, Lizz and Marisol shared a sum of money in the ratio 5 : 3 : 4. If Jean received $24 more than Lizz, how much money did Marisol receive?

21. Danielle made 800 cookies. She sold 750 of them. What percentage of the cookies did she have left?

22. There are 120 students in a school band. 45% of them are girls. How many more boys than girls are there?

23. There are 1800 students in a school. This number is 20% more than what it was last year. Find the number of students in the school last year.

24. A train took 45 minutes to travel from Town A to Town B. The average speed for the trip was 80 km/h. Find the distance between the two towns.

25. Jared had 140 stamps and Ryan had 100 stamps. After Ryan gave Jared some stamps, Jared had 3 times as many stamps as Ryan. How many stamps did Ryan give Jared?

26. Morgan paid $4.70 for 3 mangoes and 4 apples. If a mango cost 40¢ more than an apple, find the cost of a mango.

27. Bonita paid $19.50 for three books, A, B and C. Book A cost $5 more than Book B. Book B cost $2 more than Book C. Find the cost of Book C.

28. Arthur spent an average of $250 per month from January to March. He spent an average of $300 per month in April and May. Find the average amount of money Arthur spent per month during the 5 months.

29. Mr. Ross bought 20 watches for $500. He sold $\frac{3}{4}$ of them at $40 each. He sold the rest at cost price. How much money did he make?

30. When a bottle is $\frac{1}{2}$ filled with water, it weighs 2.6 kg. The bottle weighs 4 kg when it is full. Find the weight of the empty bottle.

31. Mary's savings is $\frac{5}{8}$ of Lila's savings. What is the ratio of Mary's savings to Lila's savings?

32. Kevin has 30% more books than Brian. If Kevin has 65 books, how many books does Brian have?

33. Jill sold x tarts on Monday. She sold 3 times as many tarts on Tuesday as on Monday. She sold 36 more tarts on Wednesday than on Monday. Find the total number of tarts she sold in the three days. Give your answer in terms of x in its simplest form.

34. The area of a square is half the area of the rectangle. Find the perimeter of the square.

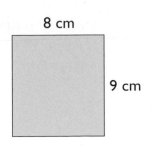

8 cm

9 cm

35. Find the shaded area in the rectangle.

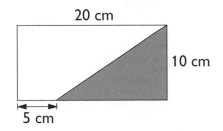

20 cm

10 cm

5 cm

36. The cardboard is in the shape of a semicircle and a quarter circle. Find its perimeter. (Take $\pi = 3.14$)

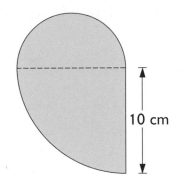

10 cm

37. The solid is made up of 3 cubes of the same size. If the area of the shaded face is 16 cm², find the volume of the solid.

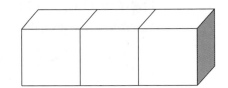

38. The base of a container is a square of side 30 cm. A stone is placed in the container. Then water is poured into the container until it is $\frac{3}{4}$ full.

When the stone is removed, the water level drops to $\frac{5}{8}$ of the height of the container.

If the volume of the stone is 4500 cm³, find the height of the container.

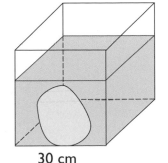

30 cm

39. In the figure, not drawn to scale, AB = BD = CD. ABC is a straight line. Find ∠BAD.

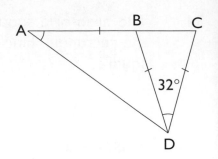

40. In the figure, not drawn to scale, AD // BC and ABC is an equilateral triangle. Find ∠x.

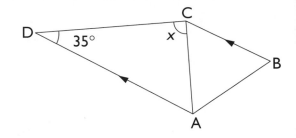

41. How many faces does the solid have?

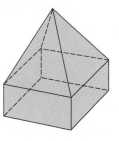

42. The pie chart represents the number of people on a cruise.

$\frac{1}{8}$ of the people were girls.

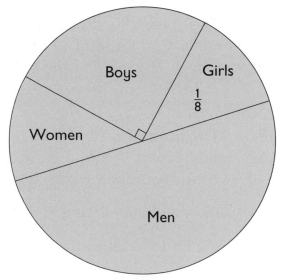

(a) What fraction of the people were boys?
(b) What fraction of the people were women?
(c) There were 120 girls on the cruise. How many people were there altogether?

6 *More Challenging Word Problems

① Whole Numbers and Decimals

1. Raju had 3 times as much money as Gopal. After Raju spent $60 and Gopal spent $10, they each had an equal amount of money left. How much money did Raju have at first?

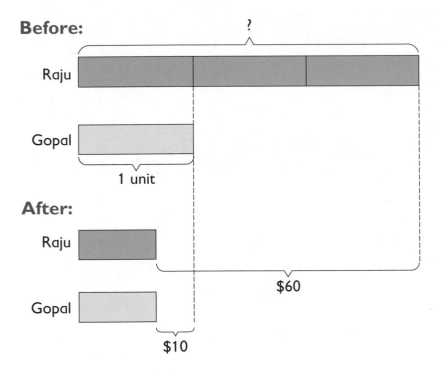

Before:

After:

2 units = $60 − $10 = $50

1 unit = $50 ÷ 2 = $25

Raju's money at first = 3 units

$$= \$25 \times 3$$

$$= \$75$$

83

2. Ali had $130 and his brother had $45. When their mother gave each of them an equal amount of money, Ali had twice as much money as his brother. How much money did their mother give each of them?

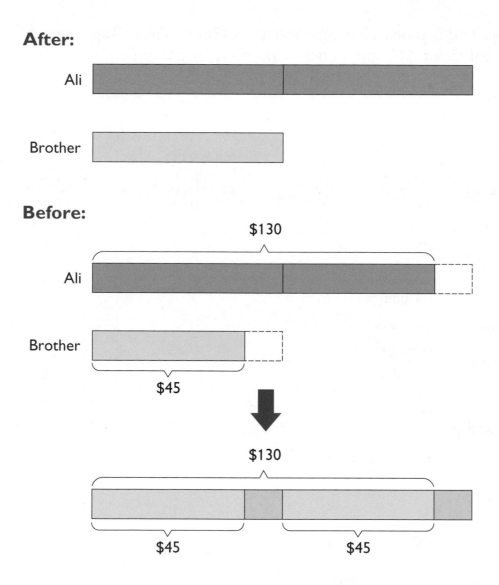

After:

Ali

Brother

Before:

$130

Ali

Brother

$45

$130

$45

$45

$130 − $45 − $45 = $40

Their mother gave each of them $40.

3. Sally is given $5 more allowance than Megan each week. They each spend $12 per week and save the rest. When Sally saves $60, Megan saves $20. How much allowance does each girl have per week?

Allowance per week:

Total savings:

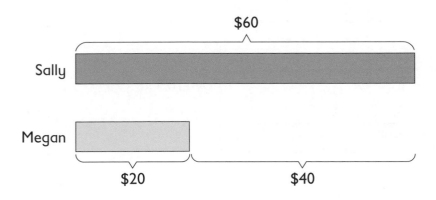

Difference in savings = $60 − $20 = $40

40 ÷ 5 = 8

They take 8 weeks to save the given amounts of money.

Sally's savings per week = $60 ÷ 8 = $7.50

Sally's allowance per week = $7.50 + $12 = $19.50

Megan's allowance per week = $19.50 − $5 = $14.50

4. The average weight of Henry, Peter and John is 35.5 kg. Peter is twice as heavy as John. Henry is 4 kg lighter than Peter. Find Peter's weight.

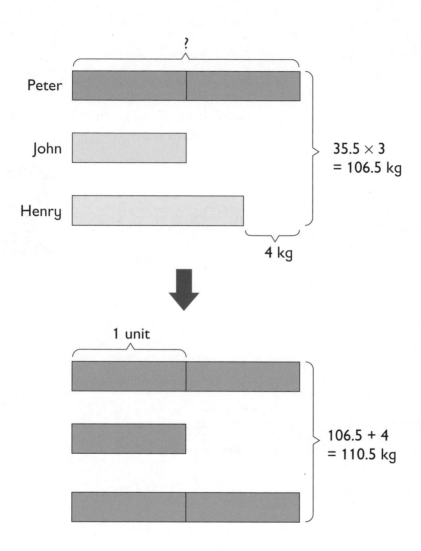

5 units = 110.5 kg

1 unit = 110.5 ÷ 5

       = 22.1 kg

Peter's weight = 2 units

            = 22.1 × 2

            = 44.2 kg

PRACTICE 6A

1. There are 148 more blue beads than green beads in a box. If another 12 blue beads and 28 green beads are put into the box, how many more blue beads than green beads will there be in the box?

2. Marisol bought 600 g of shrimps and 40 meatballs for $18. If 10 meatballs cost $1.50, find the cost of 1 kg of shrimps.

3. Melissa bought 100 mangoes for $90. She threw away 16 rotten ones and sold the rest at 3 for $4. How much money did she make?

4. A racket and 4 birdies cost $13.75. The racket costs $5.50 more than each birdie. Find the cost of the racket.

5. Rachel had 3 times as much money as Brett. After Rachel spent $9 and Brett was given $5, they each had an equal amount of money. How much money did Rachel have at first?

6. Mrs. Ward has a bag of candies for her class. If she gives each student 8 candies, she will have 4 candies left. If she gives only 5 candies to each student, she will have 40 candies left. How many students are there in the class?

7. Ricardo and Jordan had $30 and $75 respectively. After they each received an equal amount of money, Jordan had twice as much money as Ricardo. How much money did each boy receive?

8. John had 35 more stickers than Tom. After Tom gave John 15 stickers, John had twice as many stickers as Tom. How many stickers did they have altogether?

9. Damon and Eddie each had an equal amount of money. Each day Damon spent $18 and Eddie spent $24. When Eddie used up all his money, Damon still had $120 left. How much money did each of them have at first?

10. There were twice as many carnations as roses in a flower shop. After selling 50 carnations and 10 roses, there were 3 times as many roses as carnations left in the shop. How many roses were there in the shop at first?

② Fractions

1. $\frac{3}{5}$ of the beads in a box are yellow beads. The rest are red beads and blue beads. There are twice as many yellow beads as red beads. There are 30 more red beads than blue beads. Find the total number of yellow beads and red beads.

Method 1:

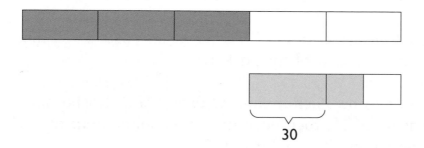

Number of yellow beads = 30 × 3

= 90

Number of red beads = 90 ÷ 2

= 45

Total number of yellow beads and red beads

= 90 + 45 = 135

Method 2:

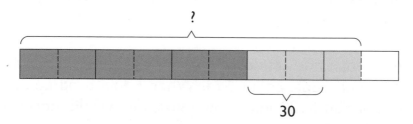

2 units = 30

1 unit = 30 ÷ 2 = 15

Total number of yellow beads and red beads

= 9 units = 15 × 9 = 135

88

2. $\frac{1}{3}$ of the marbles in Box A are blue. Box B is twice the size of Box A.

$\frac{1}{8}$ of the marbles in Box B are blue. If all the marbles in Box A and Box B are mixed together, what fraction of the marbles is blue?

Box A

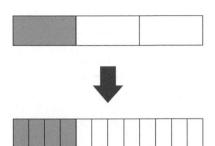

4 units ——→ number of blue marbles in Box A

Box B

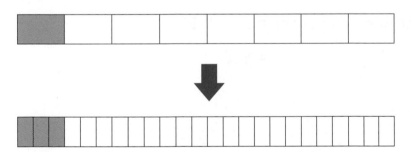

3 units ——→ number of blue marbles in Box B

7 units ——→ total number of blue marbles

36 units ——→ total number of marbles in both boxes

Fraction of blue marbles = $\frac{7}{36}$

3. Mary spent $\frac{1}{3}$ of her money on a book. She spent $\frac{3}{4}$ of the remainder on a pen. If the pen cost $6 more than the book, how much money did she spend altogether?

Method 1:

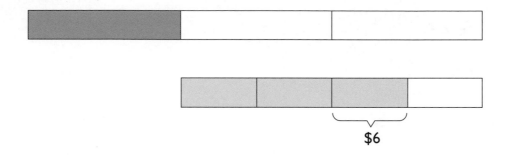

Cost of pen = $6 × 3

          = $18

Cost of book = $18 − $6

          = $12

Total amount of money spent = $18 + $12

                        = $30

Method 2:

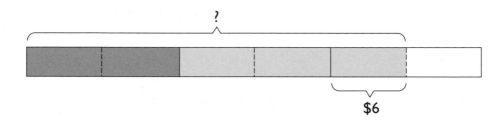

1 unit = $6

Total amount of money spent = 5 units

                        = $6 × 5

                        = $30

4. Henry bought 280 blue and red paper cups. He used $\frac{1}{3}$ of the blue ones and $\frac{1}{2}$ of the red ones at a party. If he had an equal number of blue cups and red cups left, how many cups did he use altogether?

After:

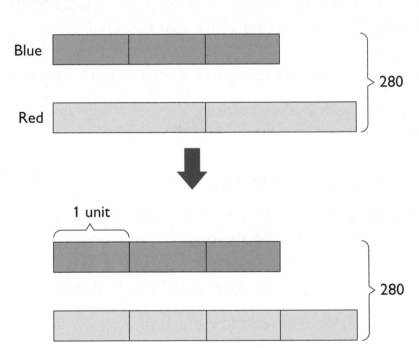

Before:

7 units = 280

1 unit = 280 ÷ 7

= 40

Total number of cups used = 3 units

= 40 × 3

= 120

PRACTICE 6B

1. Claire spent $\frac{3}{4}$ of her money on a dictionary. She spent $\frac{1}{2}$ of the remainder on a calculator. The dictionary cost $30 more than the calculator. How much did the dictionary cost?

2. Marcus bought a sweater with $\frac{2}{5}$ of his money. Then he bought a jacket which cost $5 more than the sweater. He spent $105 altogether. How much money did he have left?

3. Taylor spends $\frac{3}{5}$ of her money on 6 pots and 8 plants. With the rest of her money, she can buy another 12 pots. If she spends all her money on plants only, how many plants can she buy?

4. Thomas gave $\frac{3}{5}$ of a sum of money to his wife. Then he divided the remainder equally among his 4 children. If each of his children received $80, how much money did his wife receive?

5. Susan bought some towels. $\frac{2}{5}$ of them were pink and $\frac{1}{4}$ of them were blue. The remaining 28 towels were white. How many more pink towels than blue towels did she buy?

6. Josh spent $\frac{1}{3}$ of his money in the first week and $\frac{1}{5}$ of it in the second week. He spent $160 altogether. How much money did he have at first?

7. Carlos spent $\frac{1}{4}$ of his money on a toy car. He spent $\frac{1}{2}$ of the remainder on a calculator. He had $18 left. How much did he spend altogether?

8. Nathan spent $\frac{3}{4}$ of his money on 3 mangoes and 6 apples. If a mango cost 3 times as much as an apple, how many apples could he buy with the rest of his money?

PRACTICE 6C

1. Leigh bought a bag of beads. $\frac{1}{3}$ of the beads were green, $\frac{1}{9}$ were black and $\frac{1}{5}$ of the remainder were white. If there were 25 white beads, how many beads were there altogether?

2. Patrick spent $\frac{3}{5}$ of his money on a watch. He spent $\frac{1}{4}$ of the remainder on a calculator. The watch cost $28 more than the calculator. How much money did he have at first?

3. Philip spent $\frac{3}{5}$ of a sum of money on a dining table. He used the rest of the money to buy 6 chairs. If each chair cost $25, find the cost of the table.

4. $\frac{3}{5}$ of Mary's flowers were roses and the rest were orchids. After giving away $\frac{1}{2}$ of the roses and $\frac{1}{4}$ of the orchids, she had 54 flowers left. How many flowers did she have at first?

5. A bottle weighs 1.5 lb when it is $\frac{1}{5}$ filled with cooking oil. It weighs 3.3 lb when it is $\frac{4}{5}$ full. Find the weight of the empty bottle.

6. Juanita and Brett had $280 altogether. After Juanita spent $\frac{1}{2}$ of her money and Brett spent $\frac{1}{4}$ of his money, they each had the same amount of money left. How much money did Juanita have at first?

7. Roger spent $\frac{2}{5}$ of his money on a storybook and a magazine. The storybook cost 3 times as much as the magazine. If he had $24 left, find the cost of the storybook.

8. Cecilia spent an equal amount of money each day. After 4 days, she had $\frac{4}{5}$ of her money left. After another 10 days, she had $30 left. How much money did she have at first?

93

③ Ratio

1. $\frac{2}{5}$ of the beads in a box are yellow beads. The rest are red beads and blue beads. The ratio of the number of red beads to the number of blue beads is 4 : 5. If there are 30 blue beads, how many yellow beads are there?

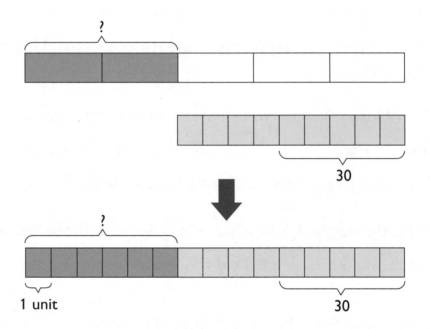

5 units = 30

1 unit = 30 ÷ 5

= 6

Number of yellow beads = 6 units

= 6 × 6

= 36

2. The ratio of Peter's money to John's money was 3 : 5 at first. After Peter's money was increased by $250 and John's money was decreased by $350, they had an equal amount of money each. How much money did Peter have at first?

Before:

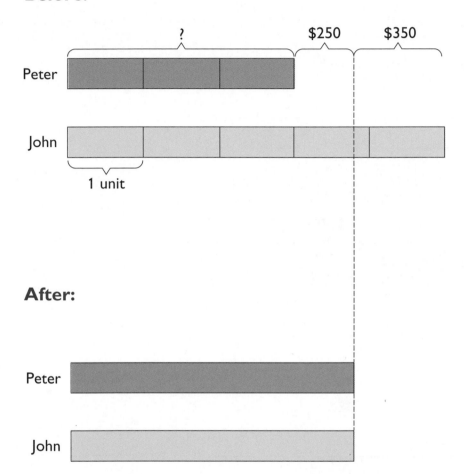

After:

2 units = $250 + $350

= $600

1 unit = $600 ÷ 2

= $300

Peter's money at first = 3 units

= $300 × 3

= $900

3. Susan's money was $\frac{2}{3}$ of Mary's money at first. After Mary gave $\frac{1}{2}$ of her money to Susan, Susan had $175. How much money did Susan have at first?

Before:

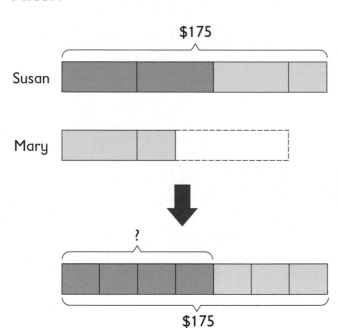

After:

7 units = $175

1 unit = $175 ÷ 7

        = $25

Susan's money at first = 4 units

                       = $25 × 4

                       = $100

PRACTICE 6D

1. Emma had $50. Jane had $10 more than Emma. What was the ratio of Emma's money to Jane's money?

2. The ratio of the number of girls to the number of boys in an art club is 3 : 5. If there are 18 girls, how many children are there altogether?

3. Peter and Salim shared 360 stamps in the ratio 7 : 5. How many more stamps did Peter receive than Salim?

4. The ratio of the weight of Package A to the weight of Package B to the weight of Package C is 6 : 5 : 3. If Package B weighs 420 g, find the total weight of the three packages.

5. The perimeter of a triangle is 60 cm. If the sides of the triangle are in the ratio 4 : 3 : 5, find the length of the shortest side.

6. Mary, Sally and Rosa shared a sum of money in the ratio 4 : 2 : 5. If Mary received $15 more than Sally, how much money did Rosa receive?

7. The ratio of the number of John's stamps to the number of Peter's stamps is 5 : 8. Peter has 18 more stamps than John. If Peter gives 22 stamps to John, what will be the new ratio of the number of John's stamps to Peter's?

8. The ratio of the number of men to the number of women in a factory is 3 : 8. There are 120 more women than men. If the number of men increases by 3 and the number of women decreases by 12, what will be the new ratio of the number of men to the number of women?

9. Pat's money is $\frac{2}{5}$ of Betty's money. If Betty gives $\frac{1}{2}$ of her money to Pat, what will be the ratio of Pat's money to Betty's money?

10. After Ian gave $\frac{1}{4}$ of his money to Juan, Juan had twice as much money as Ian. What was the ratio of Ian's money to Juan's money at first?

PRACTICE 6E

1. $\frac{1}{3}$ of Carol's age is twice as much as Mary's age. What is the ratio of Carol's age to Mary's age?

2. $\frac{1}{4}$ of Kara's weight is equal to $\frac{2}{5}$ of Holly's weight. Find the ratio of Kara's weight to Holly's weight.

3. John has $28 more than Peter. $\frac{1}{3}$ of John's money is equal to $\frac{4}{5}$ of Peter's money. Find John's money.

4. The ratio of the number of boys to the number of girls in a school choir is 2 : 3. $\frac{1}{4}$ of the boys and $\frac{1}{2}$ of the girls wear glasses. If there are 48 students who wear glasses, how many students are there in the choir?

5. The ratio of Andrew's money to Paul's money was 5 : 2 at first. After Andrew gave $30 to Paul, they had an equal amount of money each. How much money did they have altogether?

6. The ratio of the amount of water in a jar to the amount of water in a bottle was 5 : 6. After $\frac{1}{2}$ of the water in the jar was poured into the bottle, the bottle contained 850 ml of water. How much water was there in the bottle at first?

7. The ratio of the number of Jason's stamps to the number of Ashley's stamps is 5 : 2. Jason has 42 more stamps than Ashley. How many stamps should Jason give to Ashley so that the ratio of the number of Jason's stamps to the number of Ashley's stamps will be 3 : 4?

8. John had $200 and David had $180. After they each spent an equal amount of money, the ratio of John's money to David's money was 3 : 2. How much did each of them spend?

9. The ratio of Jason's money to Molly's money was 4 : 1. After Jason spent $26, Jason had $2 less than Molly. How much money did Jason have at first?

98

4 Percentage

1. A shopkeeper had 4 handbags which were of the same cost price. He sold 3 of them at 40% more than the cost price. He sold the fourth handbag at cost price. He received $260 altogether. Find the cost price of each handbag.

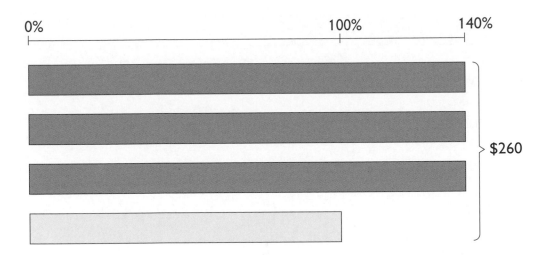

$140 \times 3 + 100 = 520$

$520\% \longrightarrow \$260$

$1\% \longrightarrow \$\dfrac{260}{520}$

$100\% \longrightarrow \$\dfrac{260}{520} \times 100 = \$50$

Cost price of each handbag = $50

2. A club had 600 members. 60% of them were males. When 200 new members joined the club, the percentage of male members was reduced to 50%. How many of the new members were males?

Before:

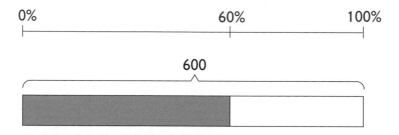

Number of males = 60% of 600 = 360

After:

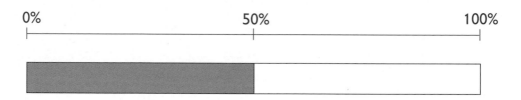

Total number of members = 600 + 200 = 800

Number of males = 50% of 800 = 400

400 − 360 = 40

40 of the new members were males.

PRACTICE 6F

1. 60% of the participants in a race were males. There were 100 more male than female participants. How many participants took part in the race?

2. Brian spent 20% of his savings on a bicycle and 15% of the remainder on a book. What percentage of his savings did he have left?

3. There are 5% more boys than girls in an art club. If there are 2 more boys than girls, how many children are there altogether?

4. Last year, Jane gave away 160 balloons to the children at a carnival. This year, she gave away 240 balloons. How many percent more balloons did she give away this year than last year?

5. Anne bought 72 stamps. She bought 27 more stamps than Betty. How many percent more stamps did Anne buy than Betty?

6. Russell has 420 stamps. 150 of them are U.S. stamps and the rest are Singapore stamps. How many percent more Singapore stamps than U.S. stamps does Russell have?

7. Tyrone gave 60% of a sum of money to his wife and 25% of the remainder to his mother. He still had $240 left. How much was the sum of money?

8. Jenny and Marvin have 836 stamps altogether. Jenny has 20% more stamps than Marvin. How many more stamps does Jenny have than Marvin?

9. Lauren spent 20% of her money on a dress. She spent $\frac{2}{5}$ of the remainder on a book. She had $72 left. How much money did she have at first?

10. Matthew had two vacuum cleaners which were of the same cost price. He sold one of them at 20% more than the cost price. He sold the other at cost price. If he received a total of $286, how much did he earn?

⑤ Speed

1. Jeff and Cameron both drove a distance of 120 km from Town X to Town Y. Cameron started his trip 30 minutes later than Jeff. They reached Town Y at the same time. If Cameron's average speed was 80 km/h, find Jeff's average speed.

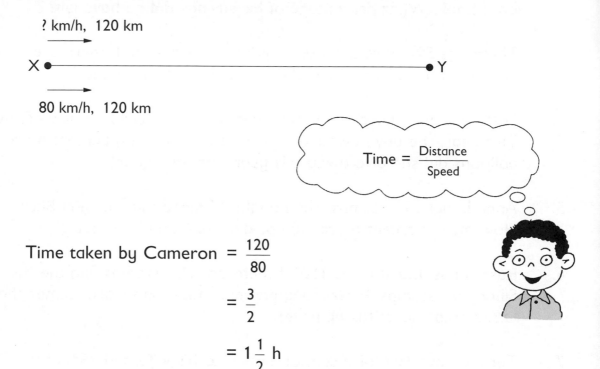

? km/h, 120 km

X ●————————————————● Y

80 km/h, 120 km

Time = $\dfrac{\text{Distance}}{\text{Speed}}$

Time taken by Cameron = $\dfrac{120}{80}$

$= \dfrac{3}{2}$

$= 1\dfrac{1}{2}$ h

Jeff took 30 min more than Cameron.

30 min = $\dfrac{1}{2}$ h

Time taken by Jeff = $1\dfrac{1}{2} + \dfrac{1}{2}$

$= 2$ h

Average speed of Jeff = $\dfrac{120}{2}$

$= 60$ km/h

2. Mr. Stone drove a distance of 80 km from Town A to Town B. He drove at an average speed of 75 km/h for the first 40 minutes. For the rest of the trip, he drove at an average speed of 72 km/h. If he left Town A at 8:30 a.m., what time did he arrive at Town B?

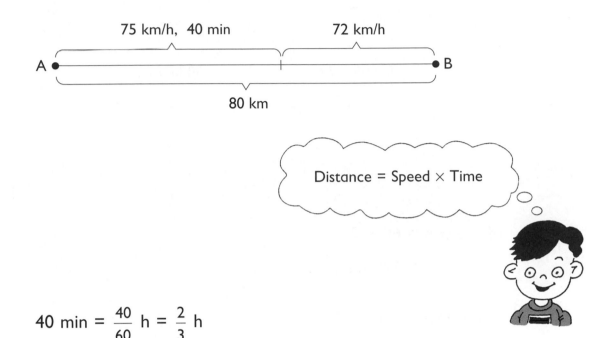

40 min = $\dfrac{40}{60}$ h = $\dfrac{2}{3}$ h

Distance traveled in the 1st part = $75 \times \dfrac{2}{3}$ = 50 km

Distance traveled in the 2nd part = 80 − 50 = 30 km

Time taken for the 2nd part = $\dfrac{30}{72}$ h

$= \dfrac{30}{72} \times 60$ min

= 25 min

Total time taken = 40 + 25

= 65 min

= 1 h 5 min

1 h 5 min after 8:30 a.m. is 9:35 a.m.

Mr. Stone arrived at Town B at 9:35 a.m.

3. Mr. Gambini drove from Town P to Town Q. He took 2 hours to cover $\frac{3}{4}$ of the trip at an average speed of 60 km/h. He covered the remaining trip at an average speed of 50 km/h. If he arrived at Town Q at 12:00 noon, what time did he leave Town P?

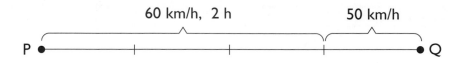

$\frac{3}{4}$ of the trip = 60 × 2

                = 120 km

$\frac{1}{4}$ of the trip = 120 ÷ 3

                = 40 km

Time taken for the first $\frac{3}{4}$ of the trip = 2 h

Time taken for the remaining trip = $\frac{40}{50}$

                                    = $\frac{4}{5}$ h

Total time taken = 2 + $\frac{4}{5}$

                   = $2\frac{4}{5}$ h

                   = 2 h 48 min

2 h 48 min before 12:00 noon is 9:12 a.m.

Mr. Gambini left Town P at 9:12 a.m.

PRACTICE 6G

1. Tina took 2 hours to drive from Town P to Town Q at an average speed of 70 km/h. On her way back, she drove at an average speed of 80 km/h. If she left Town Q at 3:00 p.m., what time did she reach Town P?

2. A van and a car both traveled a distance of 190 km from Rose Town to Orchid Town. The car left Rose Town 50 minutes after the van, but it arrived at Orchid Town 20 minutes earlier than the van. If the average speed of the van was 60 km/h, find the average speed of the car.

3. Ricardo drove a distance of 120 km from Town P to Town Q at an average speed of 40 km/h. On his way back, he drove at an average speed of 60 km/h. Find his average speed for the whole trip.

4. Mr. Jackson drove a distance of 250 km from Town A to Town B. He left Town A at 9:00 a.m. and arrived at Town B at 1:30 p.m. If his average speed for the first $\frac{3}{5}$ of the trip was 60 km/h, find his average speed for the remaining trip.

5. Nicky drove from Town X to Town Y. He took $\frac{1}{2}$ hour to cover $\frac{1}{4}$ of the trip at an average speed of 70 km/h. How long did he take to cover the remaining trip if his average speed for the whole trip was 80 km/h?

6. Mr. Banks drove a distance of 80 km from Town X to Town Y. For the first 40 minutes, he drove at an average speed of 72 km/h. His average speed for the remaining trip was 64 km/h. If he arrived at Town Y at 10:00 a.m., what time did he leave Town X?

7. Two towns, A and B, are 20 km apart. At 12:00 noon, Peter left Town A and cycled towards Town B at 15 km/h. At the same time, Henry left Town B and cycled towards Town A at 12 km/h along the same road. Find the distance between Peter and Henry at 12:40 p.m.

REVIEW F

1. (a) Round off 356,490 to the nearest thousand.
   (b) Round off 4.263 to 1 decimal place.

2. Which one of the following decimals is the smallest?
   0.6,   0.25,   0.948,   0.103

3. Which one of the following fractions is smaller than $\frac{2}{5}$?

   $\frac{7}{10}$, $\frac{4}{9}$, $\frac{3}{8}$, $\frac{5}{7}$

4. Express 0.045 as a fraction in its simplest form.

5. Find the value of $\frac{2}{5} \times 60$.

6. Find the value of $\frac{5}{8} - \frac{2}{3} \div (6 \div \frac{3}{4})$.

7. Find the value of each of the following:

   (a) $20 - (12 - 4) \div 4 \times 2$ (b) $2\frac{3}{4} - 1\frac{4}{5}$

8. What is the missing number in each ■?
   (a) $1.95 \times$ ■ $= 1950$ (b) $38 \div$ ■ $= 0.038$

9. Find the value of 3% of $25.

10. 7 out of 200 students failed a Mathematics test. What percentage of the students passed the test?

11. Kelley's money is $\frac{4}{5}$ of Tasha's money.

    (a) What is the ratio of Kelley's money to Tasha's money?
    (b) Express Kelley's money as a percentage of Tasha's money.

12. John and Trevor shared a sum of money in the ratio 3 : 5.
    (a) What fraction of the sum of money did John receive?
    (b) Express Trevor's share as a fraction of John's share.

13. Sue paid $70 for a calculator and a watch. If the watch cost 3 times as much as the calculator, find the cost of the watch.

14. Michael donated $5 for every $4 donated by Matthew. If they donated $1800 altogether, how much money did Matthew donate?

15. Susan can type 3 pages in 45 minutes. At this rate, how long will she take to type 24 pages?

16. If 100 g of ham cost $3.20, find the cost of $\frac{1}{2}$ kg of ham.

17. The average of two numbers is 56. If one number is 10 more than the other, what is the greater number?

18. Mary was given $\frac{1}{4}$ of a sum of money. The remaining money was shared between Alice and Cody in the ratio 4 : 5. What fraction of the sum of money did Cody receive? Give your answer in its simplest form.

19. The average weight of Kyle and Colin is 34 kg. The ratio of Kyle's weight to Colin's weight is 5 : 3. Find Kyle's weight.

20. The ratio of the number of boys to the number of girls in a school band is 5 : 3. If $\frac{1}{2}$ of the boys and $\frac{1}{3}$ of the girls wear glasses, what fraction of the children wear glasses?

21. Duncan spent $\frac{2}{5}$ of his money. What percentage of his money did he have left?

22. During a sale, the price of a dress was reduced from $40 to $24. By what percentage was the price reduced?

23. There are 20% more boys than girls in a computer club. If there are 44 students in the computer club, how many girls are there?

24. Duncan cycled from Town A to Town B at a speed of 12 km/h. He took 3 hours to cover $\frac{2}{3}$ of the trip. Find the distance between the two towns.

*25. A shirt cost $10 and a skirt cost twice as much. Nicole bought 2 more shirts than skirts. She spent $80 altogether. How many shirts did she buy?

26. Samuel bought a table and 4 chairs. The table cost 3 times as much as each chair. If he spent $175 altogether, how much did he pay for each chair?

27. $\frac{1}{2}$ of Joe's money is equal to $\frac{3}{5}$ of Kirk's money. If they have $220 altogether, how much money does Joe have?

28. The ratio of the number of red beads to the number of green beads in a box is 3 : 2. If $\frac{1}{2}$ of the red beads are removed from the box, what will be the new ratio of the number of red beads to the number of green beads?

29. The ratio of Emily's money to Alyssa's money was 2 : 3 at first. After Alyssa spent $30, the ratio became 3 : 4. How much money did Alyssa have at first?

*30. Kristi, Susan and Lauren shared a sum of money. Kristi received 20% of the money. The rest of the money was divided between Susan and Lauren in the ratio 2 : 3. If Lauren received $120, how much money did Kristi receive?

31. A car took 2 hours to travel from Town A to Town B at an average speed of 60 km/h. How long would it take for the same trip if it traveled at an average speed of 80 km/h?

*32. At 12:00 noon, Henry left Town P and cycled towards Town Q at 15 km/h. At 12:10 p.m., Paul left Town Q and cycled towards Town P at 12 km/h along the same road. If they meet each other at 12:30 p.m., find the distance between the two towns.

33. If $x = 8$, find the value of $\frac{2x - 7}{3}$.

34. David paid $10m$ for 3 photo albums and 2 T-shirts. Each photo album cost $2m$. Find, in terms of m, the cost of each T-shirt.

35. In the figure, not drawn to scale, find ∠x.

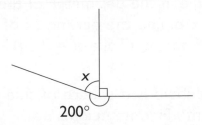

200°

36. In the figure, not drawn to scale, RP = RQ. PRS, QRT and STU are straight lines. Find ∠UTR.

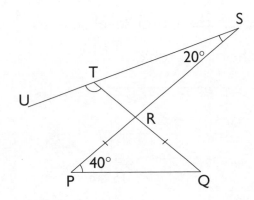

37. In the figure, not drawn to scale, CD = CE. ABCE is a parallelogram. AED is a straight line. Find ∠m.

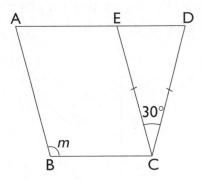

38. In the figure, P and Q are squares and R is a right-angled triangle. The areas of P and Q are 81 cm² and 25 cm² respectively. What is the area of R?

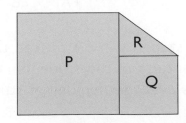

39. The figure shows a semicircular shape inside a rectangle. If the perimeter of the rectangle is 30 cm, find the perimeter of the semicircular shape. (Take $\pi = 3.14$)

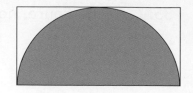

40. The base of a cuboid is a square of side 6 cm. The volume of the cuboid is 288 cm³. Find its height.

41. A rectangular tank, 20 cm long and 15 cm wide, was filled with water to a depth of 4 cm. When a stone of volume 1200 cm³ was put in the water, the water level rose to $\frac{4}{5}$ of the height of the tank. Find the height of the tank.

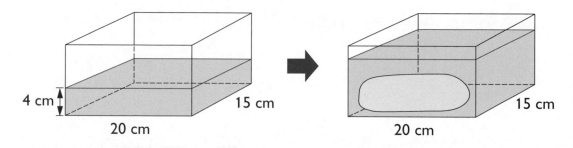

42. A school has four 6th grade classes. There are 40 students in each class. The bar graph shows the number of students who passed the physical fitness test in each class.

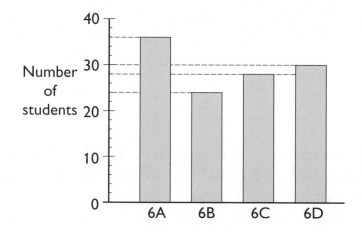

(a) How many students in 6A passed the physical fitness test?
(b) What percentage of the students in 6C failed the test?
(c) What is the average number of students who failed the test in each class?

REVIEW G

1. Write the following in figures.
   (a) Ten thousand, twenty-seven
   (b) Two million, twelve thousand

2. A number is smaller than 30. It is a multiple of 5. It is also a multiple of 4. What is the number?

3. The population of a town is about 108,000. Which one of the following could be the actual population?
   107,350,   107,802,   107,485,   107,097

4. Express 150 as a percentage of 500.

5. What is the weight of the papaya?

6. Express $2\frac{1}{6}$ as a decimal correct to 2 decimal places.

7. Which one of the following fractions is greater than $\frac{3}{8}$?

   $\frac{1}{3}$, $\frac{2}{5}$, $\frac{2}{7}$, $\frac{3}{10}$

8. What is the missing number in each ■?

   (a) $\frac{16}{24} = \frac{8}{■}$ (b) $\frac{6}{11} = 2 \times \frac{■}{11}$

9. A clinic opens at 8:00 a.m., but the nurses start work 15 minutes earlier. What time do the nurses start work?

10. (a) Express $1\frac{1}{4}$ hours in hours and minutes.
    (b) Express 2.3 km in kilometers and meters.

11. What is the missing number in each ■?

    (a) 0.8 km = ■ m

    (b) $\frac{3}{5}$ ℓ = ■ ml

    (c) 1.35 kg = ■ g

    (d) 4.8 m = ■ m ■ cm

12. How many quarters will make up $5?

13. 5 jars of jam cost $12. How many jars of jam will cost $36?

14. At a supermarket, mushrooms were sold at $0.95 per 100 g. Angela bought 800 g of mushrooms from the supermarket. How much did she pay?

15. The average age of Mary and Peter is 30. If Mary is 6 years older than Peter, find Mary's age.

16. The table shows the postage rates for sending postcards to Country A and Country B. Find the total postage for sending 3 postcards to Country A and 5 postcards to Country B.

Country	Postage
A	30¢
B	50¢

17. Kate spent $\frac{3}{5}$ of her money on a dress. If the dress cost $48, how much money did she have left?

18. Jaime, Sally and Jesse shared a sum of money in the ratio 3 : 5 : 7.
    (a) What fraction of the sum of money did Sally receive? Give your answer in the simplest form.
    (b) If Sally received $150, find the sum of money shared by the three girls.

19. Find the value of 12% of $2800.

20. A storybook is sold at a discount of 20%. If the discount is $3, find the selling price of the storybook.

21. During a sale, a store sells all its goods at a discount of 10%. Find the usual price of a basketball which is sold for $28.80.

22. Ian cycled at a speed of 12 km/h for 25 minutes. How far did he travel?

*23. Tyler bought some oranges at 5 for $1. He also bought an equal number of apples at 4 for $1. If he paid $1 more for the apples than for the oranges, how many apples did he buy?

*24. John had twice as many stamps as Peter at first. After John bought another 15 stamps and Peter bought another 60 stamps, Peter had twice as many stamps as John. How many stamps did Peter have at first?

25. A computer club has 40 members. $\frac{1}{4}$ of them are boys. If 8 more boys join the club, what fraction of the members are boys?

26. Mary spent $\frac{2}{3}$ of her money on a skirt and a shirt. If the skirt cost twice as much as the shirt, what fraction of her money did she spend on the skirt?

27. After Nicky gave Kyle $20, Nicky's money was $\frac{3}{5}$ of Kyle's money. If they had $120 altogether, how much money did Nicky have at first?

*28. David and Betty each had an equal amount of money at first. After David spent $18 and Betty spent $42, Betty's money was $\frac{2}{3}$ of David's money. How much money did each of them have at first?

29. $\frac{1}{6}$ of Jerome's weight is equal to $\frac{2}{5}$ of Donald's weight. Find the ratio of Jerome's weight to Donald's weight.

30. The ratio of Justin's money to Scott's money was 3 : 2 at first. After Scott spent $15, the ratio became 6 : 1. How much money did Scott have at first?

*31. Peter and Mary each had an equal amount of money. After Peter spent $50 and Mary spent $\frac{1}{3}$ of her money, the ratio of Peter's money to Mary's money was 5 : 4. How much money did Peter have left?

*32. John withdrew $\frac{1}{2}$ of his savings from the bank. He used 80% of the money to buy a computer. If the computer cost $2400, how much savings did he have in the bank at first?

33. Find the value of each expression when $r = 8$.

(a) $3r + \dfrac{r - 3}{5}$

(b) $2r - \dfrac{r}{2}$

34. A motorist took 2 hours to travel from Town A to Town B at an average speed of 45 km/h. If his average speed was increased by 5 km/h, how long would he take for the trip?

35. Mr. Lee took 3 hours to cover the first 180 km of a trip. He took another 2 hours to cover the remaining trip at an average speed of 55 km/h. Find his average speed for the whole trip.

*36. Chris and Chad cycled from Town A to Town B at 12 km/h and 10 km/h respectively. Chris left Town A at 8:00 a.m. and arrived at Town B at 8:30 a.m. When Chris arrived at Town B, Chad was 1.5 km away from Town B. What time did Chad leave Town A?

37. Peter drove from Town P to Town Q. His average speed for the first $\dfrac{1}{2}$ of the trip was 60 km/h. His average speed for the remaining trip was 50 km/h. If he left Town P at 6:00 a.m., what time did he arrive at Town Q?

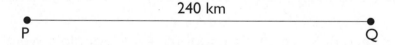

240 km

P   Q

38. John and Peter started jogging from the same place at the same time, but in opposite directions along a straight road. After jogging for 3 hours, they were 27 km apart. If John's average speed was 6 km/h, find Peter's average speed.

39. The figure is made up of 2 semicircular shapes, each of diameter 10 cm. Find the perimeter of the figure. (Take $\pi = 3.14$)

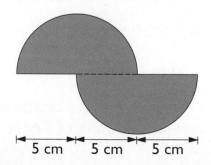

5 cm   5 cm   5 cm

40. The figure shows 4 quarter circles inside a square of side 14 cm. Find the area of the shaded part. $\left(\text{Take } \pi = \dfrac{22}{7}\right)$

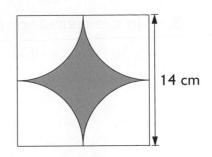

14 cm

41. The figure is made up of two squares. Find the shaded area in the figure.

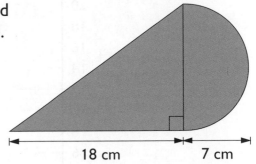

4 in.   6 in.

42. The figure is made up of a right-angled triangle and a semicircle. Find its area. $\left(\text{Take } \pi = \dfrac{22}{7}\right)$

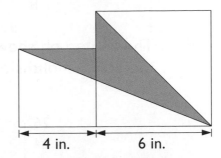

18 cm   7 cm

43. The base of an empty rectangular tank measures 50 cm by 40 cm. A stone of volume 3000 cm³ is placed in the tank. When 33 liters of water are poured into the tank, the tank is $\dfrac{2}{3}$ full. Find the height of the tank. (1 liter = 1000 cm³)

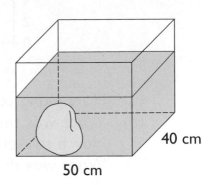

40 cm

50 cm

44. In the figure, not drawn to scale, QT = RT. PQR and PUS are straight lines. Find ∠RPS.

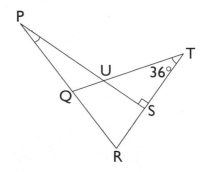

P

U

T

36°

Q

S

R

45. In the figure, not drawn to scale, AD // BC and CE = CD. Find ∠x.

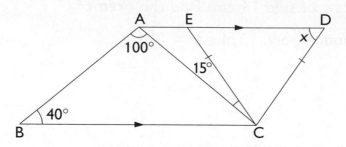

46. The line graph shows the number of computers sold in a shop during the first 6 months of a year.

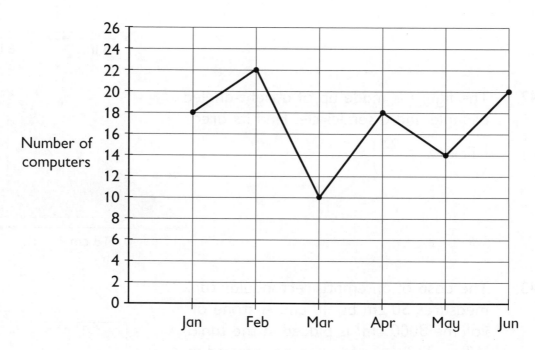

(a) How many computers were sold in February?

(b) What was the increase in the number of computers sold from March to April?

(c) What was the average number of computers sold per month?

REVIEW H

1. Find the value of the following in its simplest form.

   (a) $\dfrac{1}{8} \div \dfrac{1}{2}$

   (b) $\dfrac{3}{4} \div \dfrac{2}{3}$

   (c) $7 \div \dfrac{5}{8}$

2. How many $\dfrac{1}{5}$'s are there in 10?

3. A yard is approximately the same length as:

   (a) 2.25 ft

   (b) 1 m

   (c) 45 in.

4. Find the value of the following:

   (a) $\left(\dfrac{5}{6} - \dfrac{2}{3}\right) \div 4$

   (b) $\dfrac{1}{9} \div \left(\dfrac{2}{3} + \dfrac{1}{4}\right)$

   (c) $\dfrac{5}{7} + \dfrac{3}{8} \div \dfrac{1}{4}$

5. Divide in compound units.

   (a) 17 yd 1 ft ÷ 4   = _____ yd _____ ft
   (b) 19 qt 2 c ÷ 3   = _____ qt _____ c
   (c) 15 lb 5 oz ÷ 7   = _____ lb _____ oz
   (d) 11 ft 3 in. ÷ 9   = _____ ft _____ in.

6. What fraction of the rectangle is shaded?

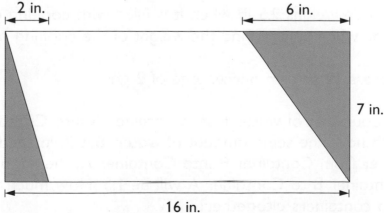

117

7. Juan had $1300. He spent $\frac{2}{5}$ of the money on a DVD player and $\frac{2}{5}$ of the remainder on DVDs. How much did he spend on DVDs?

8. Find the value of the following:

   (a) $\frac{3}{5} \div (\frac{1}{10} + \frac{2}{5})$

   (b) $\frac{4}{7} \div 2$

9. What percentage of 2 yd is 9 in.?

10. (a) $7\frac{1}{3}$ yd = _____ in.

    (b) $5\frac{3}{4}$ lb = _____ oz

    (c) $3\frac{3}{4}$ gal = _____ c

11. Find the value of the following:

    (a) $\frac{3}{5} \times \frac{5}{6} \div \frac{1}{2}$

    (b) $\frac{1}{8} \div \frac{1}{4} \times \frac{2}{5}$

12. (a) Express 5.25 lb in pounds and ounces.

    (b) Express $2\frac{5}{6}$ ft in feet and inches.

    (c) Express 3.5 qt in quarts and pints.

13. A pound of candies costs $3.60. Sally bought 2 lb and 12 oz of candies. How much did she pay for the candies?

14. A bottle weighs 2.5 lb when it is filled with cooking oil. It weighs 11 oz when empty. Find the weight of the cooking oil in ounces.

15. Express 12 pt as a percentage of 2 gal.

16. If I pour 1 pt of water from Container A into Container B, they will each have the same amount of water. But if, instead, I pour 5 pt of water from Container B into Container A, the ratio of water in Container B to Container A will be 1:5. How much water is in the two containers altogether?

17. How many cubic inches are there in a cubic foot ?

18. Which one of the following lengths is the longest?

    208 in.   6.75 yd $17\frac{3}{4}$ ft

19. Below is a table showing the amount of milk four girls drank last week.

	Amount
Sally	15 c
Taylor	1.25 gal
Morgan	6 pt
Kendra	$4\frac{1}{4}$ qt

    (a) Who drank the most milk last week?
    (b) Who drank the least milk last week?
    (c) How many cups of milk did Taylor drink?

20. Divide.

    (a) $6 \div \frac{1}{3}$

    (b) $\frac{3}{5} \div \frac{2}{5}$

    (c) $\frac{3}{7} \div \frac{2}{9}$

    (d) $\frac{7}{10} \div \frac{2}{5} \div \frac{2}{3}$

    (e) $1 \div \frac{7}{8} \div \frac{2}{7}$

    (f) $3 \div \frac{3}{4} \div 5$

21. Country A is 6325 mi away from Country B.

    A plane takes $11\frac{1}{2}$ hours to fly from Country A to Country B.

    What is the average speed of the plane?

22. Katherine has 4.5 ft of cloth. She used $\frac{1}{2}$ of it to make a curtain for a dollhouse. How much cloth was left?
    (Give the answer in feet and inches.)

23. Mrs. Baker made a cherry pie. She gave one quarter of the pie to a neighbor. She divided the rest of the pie equally among her family members. There are 6 members in her family. What fraction of the pie did each member get?

24. Which is shorter?
    (a) 1 cm or 1 in.
    (b) 1 m or 1 ft

*25. Justin had 18 marbles and Tyrone had 21 marbles. Justin and Tyrone each gave away some marbles in the ratio 1:2. Now the ratio of the number of marbles Justin has to the number of marbles Tyrone has is 3:1.
    How many marbles did Justin give away?

26. A pile of chocolate bars is 1.25 ft high. If each chocolate bar is $\frac{3}{4}$ in. thick, how many chocolate bars are there in the pile?

*27. A car left Town A at 10:30 a.m. and traveled towards Town B at an average speed of 65 mi/h. At the same time a truck left Town B and traveled towards Town A over the same road at an average speed of 55 mi/h. If the distance between Town A and Town B is 360 miles, at what time would the car and the truck pass each other?

*28. A delivery man leaves at 12 noon to make a delivery 150 mi away. He averages 50 mi/h on the trip there and spends a half hour at his destination. What average speed will he need to travel at to return by 6 p.m.?

*29. A tank is $\frac{2}{7}$ filled with water. If another 3.5 gal of water were added, it would be full. If only 2.1 gal were added, what fraction of the tank would be filled with water?